ALEX HALEY

ALEX HALEY

David Shirley

CHELSEA HOUSE PUBLISHERS
New York   Philadelphia

Chelsea House Publishers
Editorial Director Richard Rennert
Executive Managing Editor Karyn Gullen Browne
Executive Editor Sean Dolan
Copy Chief Robin James
Picture Editor Adrian G. Allen
Art Director Robert Mitchell
Manufacturing Director Gerald Levine
Systems Manager Lindsey Ottman
Production Coordinator Marie Claire Cebrián-Ume

Black Americans of Achievement
Senior Editor Sean Dolan

Staff for ALEX HALEY
Copy Editor Nicole Greenblatt
Editorial Assistant Joy Sanchez
Assistant Designer John Infantino
Picture Researcher Patricia Burns
Cover Illustrator Bradford Brown

3 5 7 9 8 6 4 2

Library of Congress Cataloging-in-Publication Data
Shirley, David, 1955–
    Alex Haley, author / David Shirley.
      p. cm.—(Black Americans of achievement)
    Includes bibliographical references and index.
Summary: Discusses the life and times of the African American author
who gained recognition for his book, "Roots."
ISBN 0-7910-1979-9
    0-7910-1980-2 (pbk.)
  1. Haley, Alex—Juvenile literature. 2. Historians—United
States—Biography—Juvenile literature. 3. Afro-American
historians—Biography—Juvenile literature.
4. Afro-Americans—Historiography—Juvenile literature. [1. Haley, Alex.
2. Authors, American. 3. Afro-Americans—Biography.] I. Title. II.
Series.
E175.5.H27S48 1993   93-16762
813'.54—dc20   CIP
[B]   AC

Frontispiece: *From his childhood in a small town
in Tennessee, Alex Haley went on to write two of
the most widely read—and debated—books in
20th-century American literature:* Roots *and* The
Autobiography of Malcolm X.

CONTENTS

BLACK AMERICANS OF ACHIEVEMENT

HENRY AARON
baseball great

KAREEM ABDUL-JABBAR
basketball great

RALPH ABERNATHY
civil rights leader

ALVIN AILEY
choreographer

MUHAMMAD ALI
heavyweight champion

RICHARD ALLEN
*religious leader and
social activist*

MAYA ANGELOU
author

LOUIS ARMSTRONG
musician

ARTHUR ASHE
tennis great

JOSEPHINE BAKER
entertainer

JAMES BALDWIN
author

BENJAMIN BANNEKER
scientist and mathematician

AMIRI BARAKA
poet and playwright

COUNT BASIE
bandleader and composer

ROMARE BEARDEN
artist

JAMES BECKWOURTH
frontiersman

MARY MCLEOD BETHUNE
educator

JULIAN BOND
civil rights leader and politician

GWENDOLYN BROOKS
poet

JIM BROWN
football great

RALPH BUNCHE
diplomat

STOKELY CARMICHAEL
civil rights leader

GEORGE WASHINGTON
CARVER
botanist

RAY CHARLES
musician

CHARLES CHESNUTT
author

JOHN COLTRANE
musician

BILL COSBY
entertainer

PAUL CUFFE
merchant and abolitionist

COUNTEE CULLEN
poet

BENJAMIN DAVIS, SR., AND
BENJAMIN DAVIS, JR.
military leaders

SAMMY DAVIS, JR.
entertainer

FATHER DIVINE
religious leader

FREDERICK DOUGLASS
abolitionist editor

CHARLES DREW
physician

W. E. B. DU BOIS
scholar and activist

PAUL LAURENCE DUNBAR
poet

KATHERINE DUNHAM
dancer and choreographer

DUKE ELLINGTON
bandleader and composer

RALPH ELLISON
author

JULIUS ERVING
basketball great

JAMES FARMER
civil rights leader

ELLA FITZGERALD
singer

MARCUS GARVEY
black nationalist leader

JOSH GIBSON
baseball great

DIZZY GILLESPIE
musician

WHOOPI GOLDBERG
entertainer

ALEX HALEY
author

PRINCE HALL
social reformer

MATTHEW HENSON
explorer

CHESTER HIMES
author

BILLIE HOLIDAY
singer

LENA HORNE
entertainer

LANGSTON HUGHES
poet

ZORA NEALE HURSTON
author

JESSE JACKSON
civil rights leader and politician

MICHAEL JACKSON
entertainer

JACK JOHNSON
heavyweight champion

JAMES WELDON JOHNSON
author

MAGIC JOHNSON
basketball great

SCOTT JOPLIN
composer

BARBARA JORDAN
politician

MICHAEL JORDAN
basketball great

CORETTA SCOTT KING
civil rights leader

MARTIN LUTHER KING, JR.
civil rights leader

LEWIS LATIMER
scientist

SPIKE LEE
filmmaker

CARL LEWIS
champion athlete

JOE LOUIS
heavyweight champion

RONALD MCNAIR
astronaut

MALCOLM X
militant black leader

THURGOOD MARSHALL
Supreme Court justice

TONI MORRISON
author

ELIJAH MUHAMMAD
religious leader

EDDIE MURPHY
entertainer

JESSE OWENS
champion athlete

SATCHEL PAIGE
baseball great

CHARLIE PARKER
musician

GORDON PARKS
photographer

ROSA PARKS
civil rights leader

SIDNEY POITIER
actor

ADAM CLAYTON
POWELL, JR.
political leader

COLIN POWELL
military leader

LEONTYNE PRICE
opera singer

A. PHILIP RANDOLPH
labor leader

PAUL ROBESON
singer and actor

JACKIE ROBINSON
baseball great

DIANA ROSS
entertainer

BILL RUSSELL
basketball great

JOHN RUSSWURM
publisher

SOJOURNER TRUTH
antislavery activist

HARRIET TUBMAN
antislavery activist

NAT TURNER
slave revolt leader

DENMARK VESEY
slave revolt leader

ALICE WALKER
author

MADAM C. J. WALKER
entrepreneur

BOOKER T. WASHINGTON
educator and racial spokesman

IDA WELLS-BARNETT
civil rights leader

WALTER WHITE
civil rights leader

OPRAH WINFREY
entertainer

STEVIE WONDER
musician

RICHARD WRIGHT
author

ON ACHIEVEMENT

Coretta Scott King

BEFORE YOU BEGIN this book, I hope you will ask yourself what the word *excellence* means to you. I think that it's a question we should all ask, and keep asking as we grow older and change. Because the truest answer to it should never change. When you think of excellence, perhaps you think of success at work; or of becoming wealthy; or meeting the right person, getting married, and having a good family life.

Those important goals are worth striving for, but there is a better way to look at excellence. As Martin Luther King, Jr., said in one of his last sermons, "I want you to be first in love. I want you to be first in moral excellence. I want you to be first in generosity. If you want to be important, wonderful. If you want to be great, wonderful. But recognize that he who is greatest among you shall be your servant."

My husband, Martin Luther King, Jr., knew that the true meaning of achievement is service. When I met him, in 1952, he was already ordained as a Baptist preacher and was working toward a doctoral degree at Boston University. I was studying at the New England Conservatory and dreamed of accomplishments in music. We married a year later, and after I graduated the following year we moved to Montgomery, Alabama. We didn't know it then, but our notions of achievement were about to undergo a dramatic change.

You may have read or heard about what happened next. What began with the boycott of a local bus line grew into a national movement, and by the time he was assassinated in 1968 my husband had fashioned a black movement powerful enough to shatter forever the practice of racial segregation. What you may not have read about is where he got his method for resisting injustice without compromising his religious beliefs.

He adopted the strategy of nonviolence from a man of a different race, who lived in a different country, and even practiced a different religion. The man was Mahatma Gandhi, the great leader of India, who devoted his life to serving humanity in the spirit of love and nonviolence. It was in these principles that Martin discovered his method for social reform. More than anything else, those two principles were the key to his achievements.

This book is about black Americans who served society through the excellence of their achievements. It forms a part of the rich history of black men and women in America—a history of stunning accomplishments in every field of human endeavor, from literature and art to science, industry, education, diplomacy, athletics, jurisprudence, even polar exploration.

Not all of the people in this history had the same ideals, but I think you will find something that all of them had in common. Like Martin Luther King, Jr., they all decided to become "drum majors" and serve humanity. In that principle—whether it was expressed in books, inventions, or song—they found something outside themselves to use as a goal and a guide. Something that showed them a way to serve others, instead of only living for themselves.

Reading the stories of these courageous men and women not only helps us discover the principles that we will use to guide our own lives but also teaches us about our black heritage and about America itself. It is crucial for us to know the heroes and heroines of our history and to realize that the price we paid in our struggle for equality in America was dear. But we must also understand that we have gotten as far as we have partly because America's democratic system and ideals made it possible.

We are still struggling with racism and prejudice. But the great men and women in this series are a tribute to the spirit of our democratic ideals and the system in which they have flourished. And that makes their stories special and worth knowing. ◕

1

SOMEBODY'S
UP THERE WATCHING

LEX HALEY PACED anxiously along the length of the pier, his tired, sleepless eyes gazing sadly across the rough, gray waves of the Atlantic. It was a windy, overcast afternoon in the port city of Annapolis, Maryland, and Haley, stopping to lean against one of the posts along the landing, was clearly exhausted.

The last 48 hours had been a nonstop shuttle from airplanes to taxis to library waiting rooms, during which the 48-year-old author had not slept a wink. But sleep was the last thing on his mind. Standing there on the dock, with the cool wind tossing the spray against his face, Haley let his thoughts wander back across the remarkable string of events that had brought him to Annapolis. He could not help but feel that it had been a miracle—perhaps an entire series of miracles—that had snatched him from his comfortable life as a successful writer in New York and set him on the whirlwind odyssey that he had just completed.

Two centuries earlier, Haley kept reminding himself, these same gray waves that now pounded at his feet had carried the crowded slave ships that brought

Throughout most of his adult life, Haley's best friend was his typewriter. An indefatigable writer, he would often brag that he spent 16 hours a day, seven days a week, behind his desk. During the 10 years that the author spent researching and writing Roots, *he became even more dedicated to his craft.*

11

the young men and women of northwest Africa to lives of bondage in the New World. Two hundred years earlier to the day, in fact—on the 29th of September, 1767—Haley's own great-great-great-great grandfather Kunta Kinte had been dragged in chains onto this very same landing, to be sold into slavery on the auction block.

Haley had discovered the news about his ancestor earlier that same day, at the Maryland Hall of Records across town. The discovery of the time and place of Kunta Kinte's arrival in America capped several months of frantic searching on Haley's part. During that time, he had traveled almost nonstop back and forth across the United States, had made several trips to England, and had navigated the Gambia River and the winding, dusty roads of northern Gambia. In the past 24 hours alone, Haley had rushed from London to New York to the Library of Congress in Washington, D.C., ending up finally in a small reading room in Annapolis. It was there that he found the information that he was seeking among the endless rolls of microfilm at the State Hall of Records.

In a real sense, however, Haley's search for his African ancestry had begun more than 40 years before, during his early childhood in Henning, Tennessee. Each summer afternoon, Haley's maternal grandmother, Cynthia Palmer, her visiting sisters, Plus and Liz, and a noisy contingent of other female relatives would plop themselves on rocking chairs on the screened front porch of the large Palmer home and trade lively, dramatic stories of their family history.

To the young boy's delight, the old women's stories were peopled with a host of colorful characters, including Uncle Mingo, Massa Waller, Miss Kizzy, Tom, and their own grandfather "Chicken George," who finally led the family to freedom. But the most farfetched of their tales—and the one that most captivated the impressionable young Alex—was the ladies' account of their great-grandfather Toby, who was born far away in Africa but had been captured into slavery as a young boy while looking for wood to build a drum.

Toby's true, African name, the women insisted against the skepticism of the other adults within earshot, had been Kintay. And each time they began their tales, the old women's speech would be riddled with a number of other strange, harsh-sounding words that Alex could not understand. As a child in Africa, Toby, or Kintay, had played a guitarlike instrument called a *ko*, and while working as a slave in Virginia, he had lived near a river called the Kamby Bolongo.

Alex was always disappointed whenever the stories would end, and he promised himself that one day he would be able to tell stories as well as his grandmother and her sisters did.

Haley had kept his childhood promise. Now in his late forties, he had become a highly respected journalist and one of the country's most accomplished interviewers. His articles and interviews in the *Reader's Digest*, *Playboy*, and the *Saturday Evening Post* were routinely read by millions of people. The *Playboy* interviews in particular—featuring prominent black figures such as heavyweight champion Cassius Clay (later known as Muhammad Ali), jazz giant Miles Davis, and opera star Leontyne Price—were generally regarded as the leading public forum for the ideas and opinions of black Americans.

And in late 1965, Haley's first book, *The Autobiography of Malcolm X*, began appearing in bookstores around the country. The book's much-heralded publication was a bittersweet experience for Haley, however. The project's critical and commercial success brought him the recognition and creative control for

In the tiny village of Juffure in northern Gambia, Haley first met his African relatives of the Kinte clan, along with the griot (center) whose stories were one of the inspirations for Roots. *"Many times in my life I had been among crowds of people," Haley would later write of this initial encounter, "but never where every one was jet black!"*

which he had worked so hard. But Malcolm X, the book's protagonist and Haley's good friend, had been murdered by a team of assassins shortly before the manuscript had been submitted to the publisher.

Instead of celebrating his own success, Haley took the time to examine his life and his career. Was he really doing what he had set out to do, he now asked himself, when he had started his career as a writer more than 20 years earlier? In spite of his success and the undeniable skills that he had acquired as a writer, he saw that there was one nagging difference that separated his stories from those of Grandmother Palmer. Over the years, he had become a master at telling other people's stories, not his own. He was growing more and more restless to tell the tale that had first inspired him to write.

Even before *The Autobiography of Malcolm X* had been completed, Haley had already begun work on his second book: the story of the rise of his grandmother's family from slavery, culminating in his own childhood in Tennessee. *Before This Anger*, as he planned to call the book, was to be published by Doubleday and, as Haley described it to a fellow journalist at the time, would be "a biography of my family, a chronicle of how an American Negro family rooted itself in this country over a 200-year period." It was a story that Haley was determined to tell.

Though much of the early work was tedious—sifting through endless record files, registries, and rolls upon rolls of microfilm—Haley discovered to his delight that it was easy enough to confirm the identities of his early ancestors in Virginia, North Carolina, and Tennessee. And by early 1966, he felt confident that most of the research for the work was complete and that he was finally ready to begin writing.

As the ambitious young writer would soon realize, however, the project upon which he was embarking was much bigger than anything he had ever imagined. As Haley was preparing to wrap up his research for the book, a sudden string of coincidences and chance encounters led him to the conclusion that to complete his story he would have to go to Africa and learn what he could about the man named Kintay, whom he had heard so much about as a child.

Not long before departing for Africa, Haley paid a special visit to his 83-year-old "cousin" Georgia Anderson, the youngest and only surviving member of the group of women from whom he had first heard the tales of his ancestors almost 40 years earlier. Her health now failing, the old woman immediately perked up upon seeing her distinguished young relative and hearing of his plans to write a book about the cherished family story.

Cousin Georgia did not seem the least bit surprised or impressed by Haley's news that through months of work in libraries, archives, and record halls around the country he had been able to confirm in writing virtually all of the family history. It was more important, she reasoned, that he remember the tales exactly as they had been told to him when he was a boy, and she enthusiastically recounted the entire saga once again, complete with the strange African words that had so fascinated him as a child, just to make sure he got it right.

What finally did make the old woman's eyes light up was Haley's news that he planned to travel to Africa, where he hoped to discover both the village where their ancestor Kintay had once lived and the name of the tribe to which he belonged. Gripping his hand firmly, Cousin Georgia suddenly seemed much younger. "You go 'head, boy!" she encouraged him. "Yo' sweet grandma an' all of 'em—dey up dere *watchin'* you!"

Before long, Haley's research led him to the country of Gambia in northwest Africa. There, he learned the meanings of the strange words that his grandmother and her sisters had taught him as a child. It was also in Gambia that he learned of the griots, the old African storytellers from the rural villages where no writing yet existed. The griots were walking libraries, Haley discovered. Each one of them had learned the entire history of the people of his region by heart and could recite from memory births, deaths, marriages, and stories of important people dating hundreds of years into the past.

Eventually, Haley traveled by caravan to the tiny, dusty village of Juffure, where he finally found a griot who could recite the legends of the Kintay clan—or Kinte, as the author learned that the name was spelled in Gambia. After hours of kneeling patiently at the old griot's feet along with the rest of the villagers, Haley was startled to hear the old man tell the story of how, 200 years earlier, a great tragedy had struck the family of Omoro Kinte, one of the key figures in the region's history. In addition to his many noble deeds, the griot explained, Omoro Kinte had fathered four fine sons. "About the time the King's soldiers came," the griot continued, as Haley looked up in amazement, "the oldest of these four sons, Kunta, went away from the village to chop wood . . . and he was never seen again."

In this tiny, remote village thousands of miles from his home, Haley had found the beginning of his

Following up on the stories he heard from the griot, Haley traveled to London, where he discovered the slave-ship records that would finally lead him to the true identity of his African ancestor, Kunta Kinte.

*Before leaving for Gambia, the author visited his beloved cousin Georgia, the last survivor
of the group of elderly women from whom he had first heard the tales of the African, Kunta Kinte.
"You go 'head, boy!" she exclaimed. "Yo' sweet grandma an' all of 'em—dey up dere watchin' you!"*

story. All that was left, he reasoned, was to put the two histories together: the griot's tale of the Kinte clan in Juffure and grandmother Cynthia's stories of the family's life in America. How did Kunta Kinte finally make his way to America? Who had taken him, and what sufferings and humiliations had he endured on the long journey across the ocean and during the period in which he was first sold into slavery? In order to know more, Haley realized, he would have to travel to England and find which of the "King's soldiers" had been in northern Gambia during the period when his ancestor had disappeared.

Haley left Juffure in a Land-Rover with the rest of his crew, his mind swimming with all that he had learned and the questions that still needed to be answered. As the truck passed from village to village, he was at first too preoccupied with his own thoughts to notice the villagers who crowded the roadside. Finally, however, one group of villagers grew bold enough to block the road, forcing Haley's party to stop momentarily. As the crowd dispersed and the vehicle slowly began to pull away, Haley could hear for the first time the townspeople crying out behind him.

"I guess we had moved a third of the way through the village," he recalled later, "when it suddenly registered in my brain what they were all crying out . . . the wizened, robed elders and younger men, the mothers and the naked tar-black children, they were all waving up at me; their expressions buoyant, beaming, all were crying out together, 'Meester Kinte! Meester Kinte!'"

"Let me tell you something," he continued, "I am a man. A sob hit me somewhere around my ankles; it came surging upward, and flinging my hands over my face, I was just bawling, as I hadn't since I was a baby. 'Meester Kinte!' I just felt like I was weeping for all of history's incredible atrocities against fellow-men, which seems to be mankind's greatest flaw."

Six weeks later in Annapolis, Haley found himself weeping once again as he stared across the waters that had brought his great-great-great-great grandfather to a life of slavery and suffering 200 years earlier. In Africa, he had at last discovered the identity of his ancestor, Kunta Kinte. But Haley now realized that he had also found an entire race of people to whom he was bound, not merely by name and by blood, but by a common history of suffering and loss. Millions of other men, women, and children had been hauled in chains across the Atlantic Ocean during the early days of America's history or had died during the cruel months at sea. And millions more, he now realized, had been left behind in their African homeland, robbed of their parents and children, their brothers and their sisters.

Standing at the edge of the pier, Haley knew that his grandmother Cynthia and her sisters were somehow there with him, watching and guiding him as he prepared himself for the task that lay ahead. But there were other presences as well. He thought of his more distant ancestors, whose stories he was just beginning to learn. He remembered the townsfolk of Juffure and those of the surrounding villages who had so graciously welcomed him back to his African home. And finally, he thought of all those nameless, faceless others who had suffered and died in silence, apart from their homes, their language, and those they loved—and with no one to tell their story.

It had taken a miracle, Haley reasoned, for a black man to learn the true story of his family—from village life in rural Africa through the long period of enslavement to a successful, prosperous life in contemporary America. It was a story he was resolved to reveal to the world.

"I feel I'm a conduit through which this is happening," he would later tell one reporter. "It was just something that was meant to be. I say this because there were so many things that had to happen over which I had no control. And if any one thing hadn't happened, then this could not have come together."

"I feel that they do watch and guide," Haley would confess years later of the powers that had led him on his project, "and also I feel that they join me in the hope that this story of our people can help alleviate the legacies of the fact that preponderantly the histories have been written by the winners." ❧

"SIS" BROOKS

Aunt E!

2

HENNING

FOUR-YEAR-OLD ALEX HALEY grasped his grandfather's long, calloused fingers as firmly as he could and tried hard to keep up with the older man's steps.

"C'mon, boy, if you're coming," Will Palmer barked teasingly at the child who stumbled eagerly at his heels. "We've got a busy day ahead of us."

It was a sleepy Tennessee morning in the summer of 1925, and the two were on their way to the W. E. Palmer Lumber Company, the thriving business owned by the elder Palmer in the small southern town of Henning. Black-owned businesses were something of a novelty throughout the country in the 1920s. Among Henning's 600 or so citizens, Will Palmer's success was regarded with genuine awe. Palmer's grandson Alex was much too young to understand all this. But little Alex knew his Grandpa Will was an important man, and the child spent every chance he got at the lumberyard tugging at his busy grandpa's coattails—at least as often as his mother, Bertha, and his maternal grandmother, Cynthia Palmer, would allow.

During the hot summers in Henning, Cynthia Palmer (center) and her sisters would sit in rocking chairs on the screened front porch and swap stories about their colorful family. It was from these all-afternoon gossip sessions that young Alex Haley first heard the tales of Africa and the man called Kinte.

23

"He's finally got that boy he always wanted," Cynthia would often say about her husband, only half kidding, "and spoilin' him just like he did Bertha." But Will was completely undaunted by his wife's disapproval. Even on the days that Alex stayed at home, Will would greet his grandson at the end of the day with a big hug and some small gift he had picked up on the way home.

"It seemed I'd nearly lost a son a little while there," Alex's father, Simon Haley, remembered years later of the day in the summer of 1921 when he and Bertha first brought their infant son home to Henning. Though the older Haley's words were spoken in jest, he may have been closer to the truth than he realized.

Like those of many future writers, Alex Haley's earliest years were spent quietly. On those occasions later in life when he reflected on his childhood, his memory always seemed to be more sharply focused on the events in the lives of those around him than on his own youthful adventures. About his own immediate family, Haley, a writer who never seemed to be short of words, remained strangely silent. It was only when writing of the early years that he spent at the home of his maternal grandparents, Will and Cynthia Palmer, that Haley's memories really came to life.

His first recorded mention of himself, in fact, was not of his birth on August 11, 1921, in Ithaca, New York—but of the time more than six weeks later, when he first appeared unexpectedly on Grandpa Will and Grandma Cynthia's front doorstep.

Since their marriage in 1920, Haley's parents had been away from Henning for almost a year, living far north in Ithaca, where Simon was finishing his master's degree in agriculture at Cornell University and Bertha was studying at the Ithaca Conservatory of Music. For several months, Will and Cynthia had heard little from their daughter and son-in-law, no

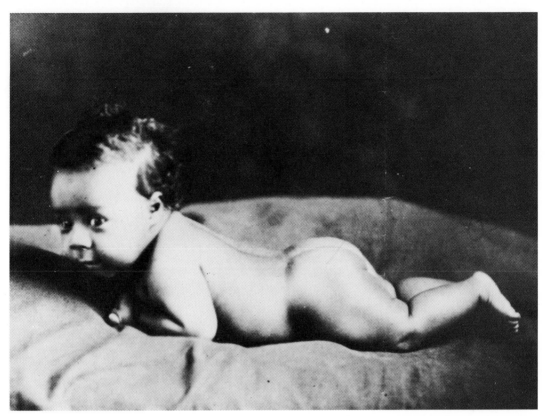

matter how often Cynthia wrote. Will begged his wife not to worry, insisting that everything was fine and that the newlyweds were probably just too busy to keep in touch. But secretly he was growing a bit concerned himself. Finally, Cynthia made arrangements to visit her daughter in Ithaca and see for herself what was wrong.

At midnight just two days before she was scheduled to depart, Cynthia and Will were awakened by a knocking at their front door. The older couple were shocked to find not two but three unexpected visitors waiting on their front porch.

"Sorry we didn't write," Bertha finally broke the silence as she handed her mother the tiny, six-week-old baby she had been cradling in her arms. "We wanted to bring you a surprise present."

Alex (above) was six weeks old when Simon and Bertha Haley first introduced him to his grandparents Cynthia and Will Palmer. "Seems I'd nearly lost a son a little while there," Simon Haley would later laugh, describing the close bond that was immediately formed between young Alex and his grandfather Will.

Haley was born at this house on Cascadilla Street, in Ithaca, New York, on August 11, 1921. Haley's father, Simon, was pursuing a master's degree in agriculture at Cornell University. A talented pianist, Bertha Haley was planning to enroll at the nearby Ithaca Conservatory of Music, but within six weeks of his birth, Alex accompanied his parents to Henning, Tennessee, where both he and his mother would spend the earliest years of his childhood.

Will Palmer gave his wife plenty of time to admire her new grandson. Then, without as much as a word, he gently took the child from her arms and walked out into the moonlit yard and around to the back of the house. Half an hour later, Will and his grandson Alex returned. No one asked where Will had taken the boy, but everyone knew that there was now a special bond between the two. "All of us knew," Alex's father recalled later, "how badly for many years he'd wanted to have a son to raise—I guess in your being Bertha's boy, you'd become it."

Will Palmer may have wanted a boy, but he certainly never lacked affection for Bertha, his only daughter. As far as Will was concerned, all the hard work and long hours were intended for her benefit, and he was determined that she, and her children, would escape the cycle of poverty and ignorance in which he and her mother had been forced to live much of their lives. From the time Alex's mother could speak, she was exposed to music, art, politics, and literature—all the things that had been lacking from her parent's lives.

To the town's amusement, the normally withdrawn businessman literally smothered his daughter with affection and gifts, including a brand-new piano for her eighth birthday, a membership in the National Association for the Advancement of Colored People (NAACP), and her own Sears, Roebuck mail-order account. Finally, after she had finished the eighth grade, Bertha was enrolled at the Lane Institute, a black preparatory school and junior college in nearby Jackson, Tennessee. It was the fulfillment of Will's dream for his daughter: she would be the first member of either his or Cynthia's family ever to attend college.

At Lane, Bertha met and fell in love with young Simon Haley, a handsome, ambitious, fair-skinned agricultural student with a fine baritone singing voice and—if the rumors were true—more than a hint of Irish blood. Like many of their peers, Simon and Bertha saw their courtship interrupted by the First World War. Along with all the other males in his senior class at North Carolina Agricultural & Technical College in Greensboro, he enlisted in the army, eventually seeing combat in France's Argonne Forest, where he was gassed. After a lengthy, impatient convalescence in an overseas hospital, Simon returned home, and the two were finally wed at the Palmer's home church in Henning in the summer of 1920. Almost immediately, they left for New York.

During his two years of study in North Carolina, Simon Haley had a remarkable encounter that helped shape his—and later his son Alex's—view of the world. With his modest savings almost completely exhausted by the end of his junior year, he had reluctantly begun to consider dropping out of college to return to sharecropping. "Working four odd jobs," he would later explain to his children, "I just never had time to study."

At the last moment, Simon Haley landed a summer job as a Pullman porter with the railroad. Early one morning, he was directed to deliver a glass

A handsome, articulate young man with a powerful baritone singing voice, Simon Haley (right) first met his future wife Bertha Palmer (opposite) at Lane Institute in Jackson, Tennessee. As her father, Will Palmer, had done for her, Bertha longed to provide her children with an even better life than she had known. She suffered from poor health, however, and would die at the age of 36, when Alex was only 10 years old.

of warm milk to the car of a sleepless couple on their way from Buffalo to Pittsburgh. Impressed with the way the young porter carried himself, the distinguished older white man who had summoned Simon asked if he would stay a while and talk. In the brief conversation that followed, the porter did most of the talking. He learned very little about the man who seemed so curious about Simon's work and his college studies in Greensboro. Nevertheless, he was happy to receive a large tip when the man and his wife left the train in Pittsburgh.

Thinking no more about it, Simon returned to his senior year at college at the end of the summer, and what he feared was a hopeless situation. His savings over the summer were still not enough to allow him to continue his education. He was shocked

to learn, however, that during his absence his tuition had been paid in full by a Mr. R. S. M. Boyce, a retired executive from the Curtis Publishing Company—the same man Simon had met briefly several months earlier on the train.

"It was about $503.15 with tuition, dormitory, meals and books included," Alex Haley's father would recite in later years, still shaking his head in disbelief. For once, given the chance to devote all of his time to his studies, Simon achieved high enough marks to earn a full scholarship to graduate school at Cornell, a goal about which he had only dreamed.

Years later in New York, Malcolm X would try to persuade his friend Alex Haley that blacks could make their lives better only by separating themselves as far as possible from the white community. Since

Serious, hardworking, and fiercely proud, blacksmith Tom Murray (right) and his wife, Irene (left), led their family from life on a slave plantation to 30 acres of freedom in Henning, Tennessee. Tom Murray was secretly delighted when his daughter Cynthia married former share-cropper and would-be business owner Will Palmer, whom Murray affectionately regarded as a younger version of himself.

the days of slavery, Malcolm insisted, whites had profited consistently from the suffering and oppression of blacks. It was a social and economic advantage that whites simply could not be trusted to change of their own free will. Like Malcolm X, Haley was destined to make his name writing about slavery and the oppression of his race; but he would always remain suspicious of those who called for a separation of the races. Like his father, he could never forget the unprovoked and unexpected generosity of R. S. M. Boyce, the retired publishing executive who forever changed his father's life and the lives of his children.

Yet it was his grandparents Will and Cynthia—and not his immediate family—whose lives and stories would have the greatest impact on the young Alex Haley. As Haley later described them, Will and Cynthia Palmer were two fiercely independent people, with sharply differing beliefs and values, but a strong, abiding love for one another.

For Grandma Cynthia, who came from a strong, tightly knit family, life's secrets lay hidden in the past.

As far back as Haley could remember, the old woman had continually hounded anyone within earshot with the family tales that she herself had heard as a child in North Carolina. For Will and Bertha, Cynthia's reverence for her past and her distant ancestors, along with her continual references to slave life and African words and customs, were an embarrassing reminder of the past they were working so hard to leave behind. Little Alex, however, was always a captive audience for his grandmother's colorful stories.

For Alex's Grandpa Will, the best of life was in the future. A strong-willed, soft-spoken man, Will Palmer believed and taught that nothing could take the place of hard work and the comfort and security that it would eventually bring to oneself and one's family. He was determined above all that, whatever it took, his daughter Bertha would have a good life. "I jes' know," he once confided to Cynthia, "I'll draw my last breath seein' she have better chance'n us did." And America, Will believed, was a land that rewarded hard work, a place where even the poorest, most destitute individual could rise, through patience and industry, to a better quality of life.

Given his own remarkable story, few people were willing to argue with him. The son of freed slaves, Will had fled his home and his dead-end job sharecropping cotton in Brownsville, Tennessee, when he was still in his teens, settling finally in neighboring Henning. For the next several years, he was barely able to make a living, picking berries, chopping and hauling wood, and doing other odd jobs he could find. All the hard work finally began to pay off when the owner of the local lumber company noticed Will's diligence and hired him as a full-time delivery boy. Instead of slowing down now that he had steady employment, Will worked even harder. It was during this period that he began to court Cynthia, who complained to her sisters that "about all Will Palmer

The patriarch of the Murray clan, "Chicken George" endured the hardships of slavery and separation from his family with a combination of stubbornness, cunning, and good humor. He also possessed a rare gift for training chickens to fight.

seemed to care about was his dreams to save enough so that one day he could open and operate a business of his own."

That day was to come much sooner than either of them expected. Will and Cynthia were married in

Henning in 1893. Two years later, about the time Alex's mother, Bertha, was born, the lumber company was in trouble. Will's boss, it seemed, had a drinking problem and had neglected the business and squandered almost all of its resources. Through it all, Will continued to work as he always had, gradually gaining the respect of the entire community. Henning's business leaders met privately to decide what to do about the lumber company, which the town could not afford to lose. Their decision was unanimous: they would step in and provide the funds to save the company, but only on the condition that Will Palmer be chosen to run the business.

It took Will less than a month to have the business once again running smoothly and profitably. But he would never forget what the town had done for him. He would always feel that he owed to others the same measure of kindness and respect that had been shown to him, and he was constantly doing favors for various people in the community. For years, no one who came into the store asking for credit was turned away, even when Will knew that they would probably never be able to pay him back.

Will was so generous, in fact, that the accumulated debt began to put a strain on the business, and he found himself having to work even harder just to stay afloat. He worked so hard at times that Cynthia began to worry for his health. "Take a vacation, you hear me, Will Palmer, for your own good," Alex remembered her pleading when he was a child. But Will Palmer, now more than 60 years old, kept working day and night, and extending credit to anyone who asked.

Finally, one morning in 1926, Cynthia Palmer's worst fears were realized. After all the years of hard work, Will Palmer died of a heart attack at the age of 62. The entire community rallied around the family, and Alex's father left school temporarily to

After his father completed graduate school at Cornell, Alex (right) and the rest of the family found themselves moving from one place to another, as Simon Haley served as dean at a number of black agricultural schools across the South. For Alex, however, Henning was the home to which he always longed to return.

take over the company. But soon there was more bad news. Simon Haley discovered that the business was in far worse trouble than Will had ever dared confide to his wife. Suddenly, Cynthia was faced with the reality that she would have to sell the business, and that even then there was no guarantee she would not have to sell her house in order to cover the debt.

By Christmastime, the company had finally been sold, but the family was still awaiting word from the bank about the fate of the Palmer home. On Christ-

mas Eve, as the entire family sat around the Christmas tree, they heard a light tapping at the door and discovered that a mysterious package had been left on the front porch. The note on the package said only that it was intended for Cynthia Palmer and that under no circumstances should it be opened before Christmas morning. The large box was so light and made so little noise when he shook it that five-year-old Alex thought it might be empty, and he wondered why anyone would play such a mean trick on his grandmother after all she had been through.

Everyone wanted to open the box right away, but the instructions were clear. Cynthia Palmer said that they would have to wait until the next morning for the mystery to be solved.

On Christmas morning, Cynthia waited patiently until all the other gifts had been exchanged before taking the last gift from under the tree. "Nervously gripping one of her pairing knives," Alex Haley later recalled, "Grandma cut the glued paper wrapping tape, and the top opened to reveal a smaller box. Inside was yet another box, and within that sat a child-size 'Buster Brown' white shoe box. Lifting its lid, Grandma hesitantly withdrew a long, brown envelope. Raising its flap, she pulled out a folded piece of paper. She read it quickly and gasped. 'The bank, it says: Paid in Full.'"

That spring, Cynthia Palmer recruited all five of her graying, middle-aged sisters to come and spend the summer with her. It was the first time they had all been together in one place since their childhood, and they spent the lazy summer days on the front porch catching up.

Five-year-old Alex had always enjoyed listening to his grandmother's colorful stories in the past. Now, for the first time, he was delighted to hear the whole Murray clan embellish Grandma Cynthia's fragmented recollections with the full force of their collective memory.

"Those graying ladies endlessly reminisced about when they'd been girls growing up in North Carolina," Alex Haley remembered of the summer that was to hold so much importance for his future, "with their freed-slave blacksmith father, Tom Murray, and their mother, Mathilda, and of their colorful, game-cocking grandfather, 'Chicken George,' who had told them of his gentle mother, 'Miss Kizzy,' who in her turn had told him of her African father who always said his name was 'Kintay.'"

Before long, all of the business related to Will Palmer's estate had been put in order, and Simon Haley returned to Ithaca to finish his degree. Upon his graduation, Alex's father took the first of many college teaching assignments throughout the South, and the Haley family was reunited at last.

The reunion did not last for long, however. When Alex was 10, his mother, who had been sick off and on since his birth, died suddenly at the age of 36, and Simon was left to raise the family alone. By now, there were three children; Alex's brother George had been born in 1925, and little Julius had come along in 1929. Two years after his wife's death, Simon married again, to one of his teaching colleagues, Zeona Hatcher. Alex's half-sister, Lois, was born a few years later.

Like his father-in-law, Simon Haley worked hard to give his children an even better chance of success than he had, and he pushed his gifted children to apply themselves as he himself had done and to take advantage of every opportunity they received. As busy as Simon was in his position as a college dean, he never missed a chance to make his point. On one occasion, when the family was living in Alabama, Simon took his sons to the Tuskegee Institute to meet the great black scientist George Washington Carver, who gave each of the boys a flower and echoed Simon's favorite message on the importance of long, hard hours of study.

In time, all of Simon's encouragement and pressure would have their effect. When Alex's father died at the age of 83, George was in the middle of a successful career in politics, Julius worked for the U.S. Navy Department, daughter Lois was a music teacher, and Alex, of course, was already a highly celebrated author.

The years following his mother's death were not an easy time for Alex. If his uncharacteristic silence regarding the period is any indication of his feelings, he never really recovered from the loss of his mother, nor would he ever fully adjust to his father's remarriage when he was 12 years old. And as Alex approached adolescence, his father's well-intentioned demands finally began to take their toll. The two often quarreled, with Alex growing more and more restless and dissatisfied with his father's old-fashioned values and endless pressure to conform.

Always a talented student, the oldest Haley boy finished school two years early with a C average, then headed for college in North Carolina the following fall, at the age of 15. One thing about which Haley and his father did agree was that after two years of college, Alex was far from ready to consider a career. And in 1939, at the ripe old age of 17, Alex quit school and left home once and for all, enlisting in what was supposed to be a three-year stint in the Coast Guard. ❧

3

AT SEA

LIFE AT SEA was not at all what Alex Haley had expected. He had left home at the age of 17 with high expectations, hoping to see the world and become a man before returning in three years to complete his college education. Instead, the sights that most often greeted him during his early years in the Coast Guard were the ship's loud, crowded cafeteria, where he worked long hours as a messboy and then as a cook, and the tight, tiny quarters to which most of his off-duty hours were confined.

The USS *Murzin*, the ship on which Haley first saw active duty, was a large cargo-ammunition vessel assigned to the vast, still waters of the Southwest Pacific for as long as three months at a time. Like many of his fellow recruits, Haley was a bit unnerved by the long, lonely nights at sea. Even after the fierce battles of World War II finally erupted in the region, he later confessed, "our crew's really most incessant fighting wasn't of enemy aerial bombers or submarines, but our fighting of sheer boredom."

In a roundabout way, it was these prolonged periods of forced inactivity that finally enabled Haley to find something worthwhile to do with himself. At first, he began to read obsessively—books, news-

Haley joined the Coast Guard at the age of 17, hoping to see the world and become a man before he returned to finish college. But the young sailor soon developed an enduring passion for life at sea. It would be another 20 years before he would retire his commission to pursue his career as a writer.

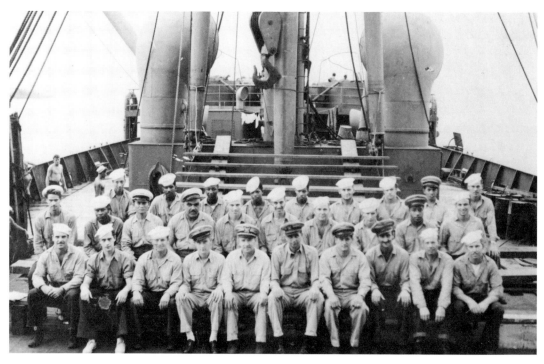

During his long, lonely missions in the Indian Ocean, Alex received his first writing assignments: composing love letters to the portside girlfriends of his crewmates aboard the USS Murzin.

papers, magazine articles, anything he could put his hands on. Quickly exhausting the ship's small library, he began to write long, elaborate letters to everyone he knew, greedy for any little morsel of news from home that his own correspondences might provoke.

Haley had become a skilled typist while in high school, and he had somehow possessed the foresight to squeeze his prized portable typewriter snugly among the small crate of belongings that he was permitted to carry on board. Not surprisingly, many of his shipmates began to take notice, at first disapprovingly, of the ceaseless metallic clatter that rang out each night from the young messboy's quarters. More often than not, however, Haley was quickly able to turn his crewmates' complaints into a friendly conversation about his own interest in and talent for writing. Soon Haley's fellow seamen were standing in line to offer their young shipmate his first real "writing assignments."

"I began writing love letters for the crew," Haley recalled, laughing fondly at his earliest days on board the *Murzin*. "I wrote flowery stuff to girls all over Australia and New Zealand for the guys."

Haley's elaborately deceitful favors for his buddies would eventually inspire his first ill-fated attempts to become a published author. Each time the crew casted anchor, he would stuff a handful of envelopes into the ship's mailbag, filled with sensationalized, sentimental love stories that he had written for popular magazines such as *True Confessions* and *Modern Romances*. As Haley was later the first to admit, the stories were dreadful, and every last one was wisely rejected by the magazines' editors.

But even though he had yet to develop an appealing style of his own, Haley had already begun to think of himself as a writer. It would only be a matter of time, he reasoned, before his talents caught up with his ambitions. And time was one thing he had plenty of on board the USS *Murzin*.

Haley's crewmates were not the only ones to notice his enthusiasm for writing or his formidable skills at the typewriter. Before long, the ship's officers began to offer him petty office assignments: typing correspondence, filing, and running a mimeograph machine. For years, Haley balanced these informal responsibilities with his duties in the ship's mess hall, still spending every spare minute writing stories and collecting rejection slips from faraway publishers in New York.

Eventually, Haley's writing talents developed to the point that he was promoted and reassigned to an office job on shore. His new rating was Chief Journalist, a public relations position that had been created by his superiors just for him, and his new station was New York City, the mecca for aspiring young writers during the period. Even in his new position, Haley's responsibilities as a writer were limited to penning speeches for other officers and working with the civilian press on rescue stories.

But the years of rejection by publishers had not stopped Haley from believing in himself, and he continued to spend his nights in front of his typewriter at work on his own projects, tirelessly teaching himself the skills he would need to survive as a journalist.

"The idea that one could roll a blank sheet of paper into a typewriter and write something on it that other people would care to read," Haley explained years later of his stubborn refusal to give up on his literary ambitions, "challenged, intrigued, exhilarated me—and does to this day. I don't know what else motivated and sustained me through trying to

write, every single night, seven nights a week—mailing off my efforts to magazines and collecting literally hundreds of rejection slips."

Over time, Haley's writing skills markedly improved, as well as did his taste in topics. While at sea, he had become increasingly fascinated with the history of the Coast Guard and the adventures of some of its heroic past crews. Gradually, he began to fashion his own real enthusiasm for the stories that he read in the ship's library or heard among the more seasoned members of the crew into his own polished tales of maritime adventure.

It was when Haley began to submit these stories to the men's adventure magazines that he and his shipmates loved to read that his luck suddenly began

Haley's considerable writing ability soon gained the attention of his superiors in the Coast Guard. Eventually he was promoted to chief journalist, a position created specifically for him, and transferred to an office in New York, a city full of young, aspiring writers like himself.

to change. During the Christmas holidays of 1949, he sold three stories at one time to *Coronet*, one of the most popular men's magazines of the day. All of the stories were on the history of the Coast Guard.

If Haley had ever had any doubts about the career upon which he was now preparing himself to embark, they were quickly erased once and for all by the acceptance letter from *Coronet*. It had been more than 10 years since he had first enlisted for a three-year stint in the Coast Guard, and his goal of returning to North Carolina and completing his college training had now become a distant memory. More than anything else, he wanted to be a writer, and that is exactly what he determined to be as soon as he completed the additional 10 years necessary for early retirement from the Coast Guard. In the meantime, he was in New York City, and he planned to spend every spare moment writing, making contacts, and peddling his work.

Haley's literary ambitions were temporarily put on hold when he was transferred from New York to San Francisco in 1954. The move to the West Coast was also significant for giving Haley, who had been so insulated as the precocious child of a black college dean, his first real face-to-face encounter with the deep racial prejudice that would preoccupy much of his later work.

"I bought a station wagon and started cross country," Haley later told a reporter of his long, harrowing trip to California. "I can't tell you how I felt after driving all day and then coming to a line of motels, all with vacancy signs, and being told they were filled up. On some nights, I had to sleep in the car. One motel let me in and charged me $20 for an $8 room. It was ironic because I was wearing a uniform with lots of battle stars. By the time I got to San Francisco I was ready to join the Black Muslims, only I hadn't heard about them yet."

Ironically, it was in San Francisco only a few years later that Haley first heard from friends of the burgeoning Muslim community back East and of its charismatic young spokesperson Malcolm X. Immediately, Haley began to collect stories and information about the movement, thinking it might make a good story once he had gained his discharge from the Coast Guard and moved back to New York.

Finally, in 1959, at the age of 37, Haley completed his 20 years with the Coast Guard. Anxious about facing unemployment for the first time in his adult life, he put his literary ambitions momentarily on hold and went looking for steadier employment in public relations. As luck would have it, his second major encounter with racism, this time among the New York corporate community, forced him to pursue a writing career whether he was ready for it or not.

During a particularly bleak period as an aspiring writer in New York City, Haley wrote letters to a number of prominent black writers who lived in his neighborhood, hoping they could offer advice or encouragement. The only one to respond was James Baldwin (pictured), the distinguished author of Another Country *and* Go Tell It on the Mountain. *Baldwin took Haley under his wing and became a major influence in his development as a writer.*

"I wanted to make it as a writer," Haley later confessed, "but I turned chicken and came to New York to find a job. I knew of other guys who had served their hitches and then gotten public relations jobs, so I made a careful resume and sent it to twenty-five of the biggest advertising and PR agencies. I put my picture on every resume—I was being practical. I got back only two replies. One sent me a form to fill out; the other wrote me a note. 'Thank you for thinking of us.'"

If agencies would not hire him because of the color of his skin, Haley reasoned, they certainly couldn't stop him from writing. "I decided to make it as a writer or else," he remembered proudly. "Just jump off the limb, go for broke. I guess I wrote 16 to 18 hours a day for seven days a week."

But even with all the hard work, it was rough going for a while. Haley found the cheapest accommodations available—a dark one-room basement apartment in Greenwich Village—and, as he later joked, he then "prepared to starve." He almost did. "One day I was down to 18 cents and a couple of cans of sardines, and that was it," he told a reporter almost 20 years later.

Broke and discouraged, Haley sought friendship and support from other writers in the community whose work he admired. At one point, he wrote to six prominent black writers living in the Village, asking for advice and encouragement. The only one to respond was James Baldwin, the highly respected author of Go Tell It on the Mountain. Receiving Haley's letter and sensing the young man's desperation, Baldwin, as Haley later remembered gratefully, "who didn't know me from Adam, came right over, and spent hours talking to me, cheering me up. I've never forgotten that."

Another, at the time less celebrated, writer whom Haley would befriend was C. Eric Lincoln. Author

Drama in Real Life®   **The Man Who Wouldn't Quit**

By Alex Haley

IN LOW tones the dean was explaining to a prospective law student the conduct expected of him. "We have fixed up a room in the basement for you to stay in between classes. You are not to wander about the campus. Books will be sent down to you from the law li-

brary. Bring sandwiches and eat lunch in your room. Always enter and leave the university by the back route I have traced on this map."

The dean felt no hostility toward this young man; along with the majority of the faculty and trustees, he approved the admission of 24-year-

54

After years and years of collecting rejection slips from publishers, Haley slowly began to see some of his work make its way into print. His earliest successes were in men's adventure magazines, for which he provided tales of daring and heroism that he heard from his crewmates or read about in the ship's library. But his big break did not come until 1954, when he sold one of his stories to Reader's Digest, *the most widely read magazine of its day.*

of *The Black Muslims in America,* the book that introduced white America to Malcolm X and the Muslim community, Lincoln would eventually become a highly respected historian and professor of religion at Duke University in North Carolina. At the time, however, he was trying to establish himself as a novelist in New York and, like his friend Haley, wondering where it all would lead. The two equally strong-willed and outspoken young men spent hours during the period arguing about religion, politics, and literature. In one of their spirited debates, Haley, only partly in jest, gave voice to the differences in temperament that would so distinguish the two men and their respective careers.

"C. Eric, that's got to be a winner," Lincoln recalled Haley roaring one afternoon upon hearing his friend's idea for a novel about the black church. "Why don't you forget all this Ph.D. [stuff], team up [with me], and make some money writing?"

To which Lincoln quickly and defiantly shot back, "You take the high road, I'll take the low road."

"So he took the high road and became a multi-millionaire," Lincoln laughed in recalling the incident many years later, "and I took the low road and became a college professor and a pauper."

At the time, however, the idea that Haley would ever become a millionaire from his writing was laughable. But he was determined to keep working toward his goal of becoming a well-known—and well-compensated author—no matter how bad things looked at the time. He believed, like his grandfather Will and his father, Simon, before him, that if one worked hard enough and long enough at something, eventually an opportunity would come along.

Haley had first begun writing small pieces for the *Reader's Digest* as early as 1954. But it was only in late 1959 when the magazine commissioned him to do a series of short biographical sketches of popular celebrities and people who had led particularly exciting lives that Haley was able to take his first real step toward becoming an established author.

At the time, the *Reader's Digest* was one of the world's most widely read publications, with more than 24 million subscribers reading the magazine in 13 different languages worldwide, and Haley jumped at the chance to reach such a broad audience. Despite the rising author's ambitions, though, most of the early pieces were light, gossipy fare, including profiles of popular entertainers and Haley's own sentimental recollections of a crusty old shipmate from his days on the USS *Murzin*—hardly the stuff on which one would hope to build a serious literary reputation.

For one of his first pieces, however, Haley dusted off his notes on the Black Muslim movement and persuaded the magazine that an interview with the fiery young minister Malcolm X would be of interest to their mostly white, generally conservative readers. The article that followed, "Mr. Muhammad Speaks," was the first honest profile of the controversial Muslim leader and the first real indication of Haley's more than formidable gifts as a writer and interviewer. The interview also marked the beginning of a close, though often strained, friendship between Haley and Malcolm X. It was a relationship that would ultimately transform the lives and the reputations of both men.

His credibility now established by the popular and critical success of the Malcolm X piece, Haley proceeded to write a number of substantive articles for some of the most highly regarded publications in the country during the next three years, including a follow-up piece on Malcolm X in the *Saturday Evening Post*. But it was not until early in 1962, when the popular men's magazine *Playboy* invited him to do a series of interviews with controversial public figures of the day, that things really began to happen for Haley.

The first of Haley's "*Playboy* Interviews" resulted from a long, informal recorded conversation between the writer and the great jazz trumpeter Miles Davis. Moody, withdrawn, and suspicious of the white establishment, Davis had long been regarded by journalists as a notoriously tough interview. But he opened up to Haley, speaking freely about his life and his music, and the editors at *Playboy* were delighted by what they read. So was the public.

Throughout his career, Haley would develop a reputation for being notoriously late on deadlines, a practice that would often strain the goodwill of his editors. With the Miles Davis interview, however, Haley's undisciplined work habits would inadvertently result in what would turn out to be one of his most significant contributions to contemporary journalism.

Haley had handled the actual interview with Davis as he always did such sessions, allowing the musician to speak freely as long as the tape rolled. Normally, the lengthy transcript of the conversation would be edited into a brief, coherent interview before it was submitted, reflecting the style of the day.

This time, however, Haley found himself facing a deadline he did not dare miss but with a manuscript that was still unedited. Desperate and not knowing what else to do, he handed in the complete transcript, hoping that the editors would at least appreciate the good moments that the interview contained and have mercy on him.

Haley first met Malcolm X in Harlem during the summer of 1959. The outspoken Muslim minister was at first suspicious of the rookie reporter. "You're another of the white man's tools sent to spy!" Malcolm snapped the moment that Haley introduced himself. But the two men eventually formed a friendship that would change both of their lives.

To his shock, the editors liked the interview just as it was and published it as the first of a ground-breaking, and ultimately trend-setting, series of free-flowing, stream-of-consciousness interviews. In many ways, the long interviews that are today so popular in magazines such as *Playboy* and *Rolling Stone* owe a lot to Haley's chronic inability to meet a deadline.

With the Davis interview and the Malcolm X profiles now under his belt, Haley soon came to be regarded as a writer uniquely suited to translate the experiences of black America into a language that white America could understand. At a time when civil rights legislation had finally begun to alter institutions across the country and racial tensions made the headlines almost every day, this was no small accomplishment.

In only a matter of months, Haley's "*Playboy* Interviews" became the day's most popular public forum for the often controversial ideas and opinions of prominent black athletes, artists, and social leaders. Delighted with the public's response to his articles, Haley continued his habit of working virtually around the clock, churning out articles and interviews as quickly as his editors would take them. In the days that followed, he conducted a series of spirited interviews for *Playboy*, including conversations with such figures as football great Jim Brown, heavyweight boxer Cassius Clay, entertainer Sammy Davis, Jr., musician Quincy Jones, and opera star Leontyne Price.

Finally, at the end of the year, *Playboy* approached Haley with the idea for an assignment that would change his life and his fortune once and for all: a completely unedited, no-holds-barred interview with Malcolm X.

4

MALCOLM X

❦

THE FIRST TIME Alex Haley met Malcolm X was in Harlem during the summer of 1959. Responding to a proposal from their rookie reporter, the *Reader's Digest* had expressed interest in a story about the Nation of Islam, an unusual branch of Islam that was gaining more and more converts across black America. Convinced that this was his big chance, Haley struck out to Harlem in search of the fiery black militant Malcolm X, who was the movement's spokesperson and, unofficially, its second-in-command.

Haley had arranged to meet Malcolm X at the Temple Number Seven Restaurant, one of the minister's favorite hangouts. But when Haley arrived, Malcolm X was nowhere to be found. Finally gathering up the courage to ask one of the establishment's immaculately dressed patrons for their leader's whereabouts, he was directed to a small telephone booth hidden away in the back of the restaurant and a tall, handsome, bronze-skinned man who appeared to be arguing with someone on the other end of the line. As usual, Malcolm X was busy at work on the community's affairs and clearly in no mood to be

"It was always a strange and moving experience to walk with Malcolm X in Harlem," wrote journalist M. S. Handler. "He was known to all. People glanced at him shyly. Their affection for Malcolm was inspired by the fact that although he had become a national figure, he was still a man of the people who, they felt, would never betray them."

disturbed by an eager young writer seeking a story—not even if the writer happened to be black.

Earlier in the year, CBS-TV had aired a special about the movement, "The Hate That Hate Produced." The television program presented a highly sensationalized, one-sided account of the Nation of Islam as an angry, separatist, potentially violent movement. The program had been put together without the full cooperation of the Black Muslim leadership.

As one who had always worked to promote and protect the good name of the movement and its leader, the Honorable Elijah Muhammad, Malcolm X felt angry and betrayed by the documentary and the hateful image it presented of his brothers and sisters in the movement. Previously reluctant to talk with the press, he was now openly hostile to reporters who dared to approach him—far more hostile than Haley had realized when he suggested doing the interview. "You're another one of the white man's tools sent to spy!" Malcolm X snapped at Haley the moment the two were introduced.

As Haley would later learn, it was a strategy Malcolm X often used to frighten away curiosity seekers and others he feared were trying to use him. But Haley stood his ground, showing Malcolm X a letter from the editors of *Reader's Digest* stating that the magazine planned to do an objective account of the movement—one that would balance what the Black Muslims said about themselves and what their attackers said about them. If Malcolm X wanted to make sure that his views were fairly represented to the public, insisted Haley, then this was his chance.

Malcolm X then snorted, Haley later remembered, "that no white man's promise was worth the paper it was on."

Once again, Haley refused to be intimidated. How could a journalist be expected to get the story right,

A small, gentle, soft-spoken man, the Honorable Elijah Muhammad (left) held absolute power over his followers in the Nation of Islam, including Malcolm X. Haley was forced to secure the permission of the Muslim leader each time he did an interview with Malcolm X.

he asked, if the Black Muslim community kept refusing to cooperate? Finally, Malcolm X gave his reluctant consent to do the interview if, and only if, Elijah Muhammad, the movement's leader, approved of the idea. In the meantime, Haley was invited to attend some of the meetings at Harlem Temple Number Seven, where Malcolm X presided, and to speak freely with the temple members.

As soon as he could arrange it, Haley flew to Temple Number One in Chicago to meet with Elijah Muhammad. To his surprise, Haley found the movement's leader to be a small, gentle, soft-spoken man in failing health, but as guarded and suspicious of the press as his second-in-command. At the time, however, *Reader's Digest* enjoyed the largest circulation in the county. Haley's journalistic piece promised exposure that Muhammad realized the movement desperately needed to get its message across to the public. Upon Haley's return to New York, Malcolm X informed him that he had been given permission to do the interview, and the two men began a series of conversations that would link them for the next several years.

Haley's article, "Mr. Muhammad Speaks," appeared in *Reader's Digest* the following year, giving white America its first objective profile of the Black Muslim movement and its brash, militant spokesperson. Virtually every other major publication quickly followed suit, with profiles of Malcolm X appearing in *Life, Look, Newsweek, Time,* and yet another piece by Haley, along with white colleague Al Balk, in the *Saturday Evening Post.* But it was not until *Playboy* brought Haley and Malcolm X together in 1962, as a part of the writer's highly celebrated, ongoing series of interviews with noted black personalities, that America got its first close, uncensored look at Malcolm X.

By that time, Malcolm had developed a grudging respect for his future biographer. But before either man would agree to do the piece for *Playboy,* the magazine had to promise in advance to print "verbatim" whatever answers Malcolm X decided to give to Haley's questions, however controversial or disturbing. It was a request to which the editors at *Playboy,* a magazine that had made its reputation and its fortune by shocking the public, were all too eager to give their consent. But Malcolm X still had his doubts. On several occasions during the lengthy interview, Haley later remembered, "Malcolm X repeatedly exclaimed, after particularly blistering anti-Christian or anti-white statements: 'You know that devil's not going to print that!'"

The magazine printed every last word of it, however, and the article quickly became the talk of the nation. An editor at Grove Press, a publishing house known at the time for its controversial and trend-setting books, was so impressed with the article's appeal that he soon approached Haley and his agent Paul Reynolds about the possibility of expanding the conversations with Malcolm X into a book-length autobiography.

This was in early 1963, and Haley had just begun his research for another major project, the story of his own family's rise from slavery. He was already beginning to resent the time and energy that the articles and interviews were taking from the story of his family, and he realized that a book with Malcolm X would completely bring his plans for his own book to a halt.

But Haley also recognized the importance of the project he had been offered by Grove. Malcolm X, Haley had learned in the brief time he had known him, was an extraordinary man, with powerful convictions and a revolutionary vision for his people. In his powerful persona, he embodied the pride, hope, fear, and contradictions of his race and of his country. For more and more people, the story of Malcolm X represented the story of the promise of the American dream and the tragedy of that dream unfulfilled. And here, just four years out of the Coast Guard, Haley was being offered the chance to tell that story to the world. It was an offer he could not refuse.

As Haley began to outline his plans for a book about Malcom X, he began to realize just how little he actually knew about the man he had made his reputation writing about. "All that I really knew," he had confessed to his future editor, "was that I had heard Malcolm X refer in passing to his life of crime and prison before he became a Black Muslim; that several times he had told me: 'You wouldn't believe my past,' and that I had heard others say that at one time he had peddled dope and women and committed armed robberies."

The two men's initial discussion of the offer from Grove was reminiscent of their first encounter before the *Reader's Digest* interview. Malcolm X initially balked at the idea before giving his reluctant consent. Once again, the final decision was left to Muhammad, whom Haley met this time in Phoenix. The aging religious leader had recently moved to Arizona because of his deteriorating health, and he coughed and wheezed throughout his meeting with Haley before finally giving his approval. "Allah approves," he pronounced to the writer's great relief. "Malcolm is one of my most outstanding ministers."

As for Malcolm X, he seemed to be genuinely moved—and somewhat disturbed—by the proposal, surprising Haley with "a startled look" when he first heard the idea. At this point, Haley knew nothing of the growing resentment of Malcolm X's celebrity among many of the Nation's members, including Elijah Muhammad, and the danger that any additional publicity might bring him. Nor could the writer fully appreciate just how much anxiety such an intensely personal project would cause a man who had spent much of his adult life hiding his past. Nevertheless, despite the risks and the discomfort, Malcolm X was drawn to the idea. "I'll agree," he explained to Haley. "I think my life story may help people to appreciate better how Mr. Muhammad salvages black people."

Of course, there were conditions. As with the *Playboy* interview, Malcolm X was to retain complete control of the book's contents. "Nothing," he wrote to Haley, "can be in this book's manuscript that I didn't say, and nothing can be left out that I want in it."

As for money, Malcolm X was emphatic that every penny he made from the book should go directly to Elijah Muhammad and his Temple Number Two in Chicago. It was crucial that no one got the impression that a minister of the Nation of Islam would profit personally from the white-owned and white-controlled media. And lest anyone still might doubt his motives in undertaking the project, Malcolm X handed Haley the following dedication on the day he signed the contract: "This book I dedicate to The Honorable Elijah Muhammad, who found me here in America in the muck and mire of the filthiest civilization and society on this earth, and pulled me out, cleaned me up, and stood me on my feet, and made me the man that I am today."

Predictably, things started badly between the two men. Malcolm X had second thoughts about the project even before the first scheduled interview, and he had little time to meet with Haley, even when he wished to be cooperative. From the beginning, Malcolm was afraid that the Federal Bureau of Investigation (FBI) had bugged Haley's writing studio in Greenwich Village, and he seemed at times to direct his angry comments not to Haley but to the imagined listeners in the next apartment or the van across the street. "For the first several weeks," Haley later recalled, "he never entered the room where we worked without exclaiming, 'testing, testing—two, three . . .'"

Another recurring problem was Malcolm X's distaste for his collaborator's success in and comfort with the predominantly white publishing world, as well as Haley's unapologetic friendships with many of his white colleagues. As a minister of the Nation of Islam, Malcolm X taught and believed that whites were devils and were not to be trusted. Blacks, he insisted, could only gain freedom, security, and self-respect by separating themselves from the white world. And here was his brother Alex, an increasingly celebrated journalist for such mainstream white publications as *Playboy*, *Reader's Digest*, and the *Saturday Evening Post*.

> Friday 9 AM - April 25, 1964
>
> جدة – المملكة العربية السعودية
>
> Dear Alex Haley:
>
> I have just completed my pilgrimage (Hajj) to the Holy City of Mecca, the Holiest City in Islam, which is absolutely forbidden for non-believers even to rest their eyes upon. There were over 200,000 pilgrims there, at the same time. This pilgrimage is to the Muslim, as important as is going to "Heaven" to the Christian. I doubt if there have been more than ten Americans to ever make this pilgrimage. I know of only two others who have actually made the Hajj (and both of them are West Indian). Mr. Muhammad and two of his sons made what is known as "Omra" (the pilgrimage or "visit" to Mecca outside of the Hajj season). I think I'm the first American born Negro to make the actual Hajj --- and if I'm not the

It is considered a sacred duty for each able-bodied Muslim man to visit the holy city of Mecca at least once during his lifetime. His trip to Mecca forced Malcolm and his biographer Haley to revise drastically the contents of the book that they had been writing together, as this letter from Malcom to Haley begins to explain.

To Malcolm X, Haley's ambition and personal success were an outright betrayal of his race. It was a conviction he found harder and harder to conceal. "Sitting right there and staring at me," Haley later recalled in horror of these recurring confrontations that threatened to end the project, "was the fiery Malcolm X who could be as acid toward Negroes who angered him as he was against whites in general. On television, in press conferences, and at Muslim rallies, I had heard him bitterly attack other Negro writers as 'Uncle Toms,' 'yard Negroes,' 'black men in white clothes.'"

Haley's military service and Christian faith were also bones of contention for Malcolm X. "He often jeered publicly at these affiliations for Negroes," Haley remembered. But for the first several interviews, the biggest obstacle to the project was Malcolm X's refusal to talk about anything apart from his involvement in the Nation of Islam and his devotion to Elijah Muhammad. Haley persisted, listening patiently to Malcolm X's informal sermons and rushing to meet with the Black Muslim minister whenever and wherever his hectic schedule would allow.

The breakthrough finally came late one night, as an exhausted Malcolm X nervously paced the floor delivering an angry tirade against a group of black ministers who had recently criticized Muhammad in the press. Desperate to change the topic, Haley asked Malcolm X to talk for a while about his mother. "Abruptly he quit pacing," Haley later remembered, "and the look he shot at me made me sense that somehow the chance question had hit him. When I look back at it now, I believe I must have caught him so physically weak that his defenses were vulnerable."

Whatever it was that persuaded Malcolm X to open up to Haley that night, the change was permanent. The two men spent the next year, whenever their schedules would allow, talking at length about Malcolm X's troubled past. Late into the night, the normally reticent minister would muse for hours on end about his proud, self-sacrificing mother, Louise, and his father, the Reverend Earl Little, a Baptist minister and social activist who, Malcolm X claimed, was murdered for his outspoken opinions on racial issues. As Haley listened in amazement, Malcolm X described his troubled, restless childhood in Lansing, Michigan, as Malcolm Little; his early days as a hipster in Boston; and his gradual descent into a life of violence and crime on the streets of Harlem. He told of his arrest and imprisonment for robbery, and of his slow, arduous process of self-education while in prison, and his eventual, life-changing encounter with the faith of Islam and the teachings of the Honorable Elijah Muhammad.

But Malcolm X's story was changing even as he opened up to Haley about his past. Two things in particular began to occupy his time and his attention. For one, the jealousy among Malcolm X's brothers and sisters in the Black Muslim community had, as he feared, begun to escalate. Even Muhammad had become openly critical of his chief disciple, silencing Malcolm on one occasion for his misuse of the press and then removing him from his position of authority in New York.

But more significant for Malcolm X personally was his deepening faith in and commitment to Islam, and the doubts that he had begun to develop about Elijah Muhammad's teachings. As Malcolm X slowly discovered, the separatist ideas that he learned from his mentor, and that he himself had preached from the pulpit, were in sharp contrast to the message of one universal family that was shared by the Muslims of mother Africa. To Muslims throughout the world, Malcolm X's pilgrimage to Mecca later that year represented a symbolic break with the authority of Elijah Muhammad and his version of Islam.

When Malcolm returned from Mecca, he had a new name, El-Hajj Malik El-Shabbazz, and he was beginning to fear that his former teacher, the man who had lifted him out of ignorance and imprisonment, was a fraud and an opportunist. And because of the angry reaction of Muhammad and many of his followers to Malcolm X's new ideas, he also began to fear for his life.

From the time of his trip to Mecca until the end of his life, Malcolm X was at the center of world news.

Increasingly, he and Haley found less and less opportunities to meet. And when they did, the conversation was usually dominated by the pressures and frustrations of the day. On one such occasion, Malcolm X, who had originally intended to donate all of the proceeds from the book to the Nation of Islam, was compelled to ask Haley to request from the publisher an advance against the royalties from the book. Cut off from the community he had spent most of his life serving, he was no longer able to support his family.

Malcolm X was also finding it harder and harder to find his place within the civil rights movement that was sweeping the country. In January 1965, Haley called Malcolm X from a pay telephone at Kennedy Airport in New York. Haley told Malcolm X that his younger brother George had just been elected state senator in Kansas, and the two men talked openly about what Malcolm X considered a dubious honor. "Tell your brother for me," Malcom X cautioned his friend, "to remember us in the alley. Tell him that he and all of the other moderate Negroes who are getting somewhere need to always remember that it was us extremists who made it possible."

Later that day, the two resumed their conversation in a parking lot, and Malcolm X continued to speak of his frustration at being excluded from and unrecognized by the movement he had done so much to create. As Haley later remembered, "He said 'the so-called moderate' civil-rights organizations avoided him as 'too militant' and 'the so-called militants' avoided him as 'too moderate.'" "They won't let me turn the corner!" Haley later recorded Malcolm X's frustration, "I'm caught in a trap!"

It was the last time Haley would see Malcolm X alive. Barely a month later, on Sunday, February 16, 1965, Malcolm X informed Haley in a telephone conversation that he had recently been given the names of five Black Muslims who had been chosen to kill him. Five days later, Malcolm X was killed by a team of assassins as he stepped to the podium at the Audubon Ballroom in Harlem.

Malcolm X had his doubts about who was actually stalking him. The U.S. State Department was reportedly dismayed by his call for solidarity between American blacks and their brothers and sisters in the emerging Third World nations of Africa, and he had long expected violent reprisal from some white racist group or at the hands of the FBI or the Central Intelligence Agency (CIA).

But whoever was responsible for Malcolm X's death, his life-long fear that he would die a violent death like his father had finally come to pass. In one of their final conversations for the book, Malcolm X had told Haley, "I do not expect to live long enough to read this book in its finished form." He was right. He was assassinated only two weeks after the manuscript was finished and almost 10 months before *The Autobiography of Malcolm X, as Told to Alex Haley* first appeared in bookstores.

But Malcolm X was wrong about one thing: his fear that he would be remembered only as a preacher of hatred and division. Along with the publishers, Haley had fulfilled his promise and given the last word to Malcolm X. At the end of the book, Malcolm X envisioned a new movement in which all races, working together "as human beings," were called to embrace "the obligation, the responsibility, of helping to correct America's human problem. The well-meaning white people . . . had to combat, actively and directly, the racism in other white people. And the black people had to build within themselves much greater awareness that along with equal rights there had to be the bearing of equal responsibilities."

When Malcolm X and Haley had first embarked on the project two years earlier, the Black Muslim minister had demanded of his collaborator that he wanted "a writer . . . not an interpreter." In many ways, Haley was exactly that, chronicling Malcolm X's beliefs and reminiscences almost verbatim, even when they were directed angrily at him.

Haley was so successful, in fact, in keeping himself and his opinions out of the way that, at the time of the book's initial printing, his name did not even appear on the front cover. That omission, however, would soon be corrected, after Haley's next project would make him one of the best-known authors in the world. ✥

"I do not expect to live long enough to read this book in its finished form," Malcolm X had told Haley in the interview for the final chapter of the book. His words proved tragically prophetic when he was assassinated during a speech at the Audubon Ballroom in Harlem on February 21, 1965—almost 10 months before the Autobiography of Malcolm X first appeared in bookstores across the United States.

5

SEARCHING FOR ROOTS

———— •(•)• ————

A LEX HALEY FIRST came up with the idea for an article about the history of his maternal grandmother's family while he was still working as a messboy on the USS *Murzin*. Throughout his childhood, he had spent his summers in Henning with his Grandma Cynthia, and the old woman never ceased to bend his ear with the tales of her ancestors—Chicken George, Miss Kizzy, and the African known only as Kintay—every chance she got. But as Alex grew older, Cynthia Palmer's colorful stories began to sound less interesting, and less believable, than they had to the more impressionable ears of a little boy.

Sensing this, the aging matriarch had one day taken her teenage grandson aside and told him to pay close attention to what she had to say. Years later, Haley still remembered the day vividly. He had been sitting by the kitchen window, admiring the tray full of biscuits that she was preparing to bake, when she suddenly called out to him, "Boy, sit down. You need to know where you come from."

This time, she talked on and on for hours, stressing with each tale she told and each character she

Will and Cynthia Palmer (pictured here with Haley's mother, Bertha, right) were the most influential figures in Haley's childhood. Together they represented the two great themes of the author's life and work. From grandfather Will, Haley inherited his burning desire to achieve, to raise himself and his people to a better quality of life. From grandmother Cynthia, he learned the importance of the past as a source of wisdom, inspiration, and community.

described that these were not just colorful stories meant to entertain. The stories that she and her sisters were always telling represented, she insisted, the history of their people and the collective memory of their family and their race—Alex's family and Alex's race. If that memory was not to be lost once and for all, then he would have to remember all that he had been told and tell it to his children and his children's children, just as she had done. It was the first time Haley had felt within him a sense of his place in his family and in the world, and the feeling that the two might somehow be related.

"I've been told our history over and over again through the years," Haley explained proudly to an interviewer almost 30 years later concerning the origins of his own early interest in writing. "Storytelling was our family's television. We've been lucky enough to have a storyteller in each generation. I guess it's me now."

A few years after his "awakening" at his grandmother's side, during the lonely nights at sea, Haley began to turn his grandmother's stories over and over in his head. Why not, he wondered to himself, preserve those stories once and for all in written form? And wouldn't the saga of an American family raising itself over two centuries from slavery to affluence and respectability be of interest to more people than just his immediate family?

The idea, however, that the tale might actually find its way back to the dark African past where it all began was, as Haley would later confess, something that the aspiring writer "wasn't all that fired up about." Haley cherished the stories that he learned from Grandmother Palmer, but the little he knew about Africa he had picked up, like most Americans of his generation, from Tarzan movies and *National Geographic* magazines. Like his parents and his Grandpa Will before him, he found the notion that

the Dark Continent of jungles and savages was somehow tied together with his own past both distasteful
and embarrassing.

And besides, he rationalized to himself, Cynthia
Palmer's memories of the African named Kintay—
who lived near a river known as the Kamby Bolongo,
called a guitar a ko, and had wandered into the forest
to chop wood for a drum he planned to make when
he was captured into slavery as a child—were far too
distant to be reliable. It was not that he did not trust
his grandmother. "You just *didn't* not believe my
grandmother," he later explained.

But Alex Haley was, after all, a writer by profes-
sion and by temperament. And, like most writers, he
believed strongly, almost religiously, in the authority
of the written word. Two hundred years and seven
generations were much too long for a story that had
never actually been written down to retain any degree
of accuracy. Certainly, he conceded, the tales that
his grandmother and her sisters told were based on
people who really lived and things that really happened. But the names, the words, and the details had,
he believed with equal certainty, been far too dis-
torted by time and the imperfections of memory for
anyone ever to match them with the records of the
family's remote African past—if such records existed
at all.

During Haley's early years working as a writer in
New York City, his idea for developing the story of
his own family kept getting pushed aside by other,
less ambitious projects. In many ways, it was the
experience of writing the book with Malcolm X that
convinced Haley that the time had finally come for
him to begin the project in earnest. For years, Haley
had worked to establish himself in the predominantly
white literary world, doing everything in his power
to minimize the role that race played in the way his
work was received. Haley wanted to be respected as

THE ROSETTA STONE

While on assignment in London, Haley visited the British museum and the famous Rosetta Stone, which scholars had used to decipher the mysterious hieroglyphics of ancient Egypt. The story of the stone inspired Haley to seek someone who could translate the African words that he had heard from his grandmother when he was a child.

a writer and as a man, not simply as a black writer and a black man.

From the beginning of his relationship with Malcolm X, however, Haley was fascinated by the Black Muslim minister's keen awareness of the powerful role that race played throughout society and in the life of his people. For Malcolm X, as it had been for Cynthia Palmer, being black was not an obstacle to be overcome but a source of identity and pride. If Haley was ever to know who he was and where he was going, he had to find a way to discover—and to embrace—his own past. That was what he had demanded of his friend Malcolm X throughout the long, often painful series of interviews that became the text for *The Autobiography of Malcolm X*. And now he was about to demand the same thing of himself.

Haley originally intended to call the book that he was planning to write *Before This Anger*. As he told an interviewer in February 1966, shortly after the publication of *The Autobiography of Malcolm X*, the book was to be "a biography of my family, a chronicle of how an American Negro family rooted itself in this country over a 200 year period."

All that changed later in the year, when Haley was sent by one of his editors to research a story in England. While staying in London, he decided to visit the British Museum, where the Rosetta Stone, which had yielded the first clue to the decipherment of Egyptian hieroglyphics, was on display. Something about the great black slab of engraved stone and its history captivated him, and sent his mind reeling back to his grandmother's stories and the strange, indecipherable words she often used to tell him. It was all he could do, in fact, to keep his attention focused on the remarkable story that the museum's tour guide was patiently relating to the crowd.

Discovered by Napoleon's army in the Nile Delta in 1799, the Rosetta Stone contained three parallel texts: one in Greek, one in Egyptian hieroglyphics, and the third in a previously unknown language. For many years, scholars around the world assumed that the three texts told three totally different stories, and that the unrecognizable language and the hieroglyphic message would probably never be translated successfully.

A French Egyptologist named Jean Champollion defied the conventional wisdom that the stone contained three separate messages and eventually used the Greek text to translate the other two. Champollion's controversial research represented the most significant archaeological discovery of his era, enabling future scholars to decipher for the first time the strange, comic book–like illustrations that line the walls of the ancient pyramids and giving the world its first real glimpse into the mysteries of ancient Egyptian civilization.

Suddenly, right in the middle of the tour guide's address, everything became clear to Haley. If Jean Champollion could use the language of ancient Greece to decode Egyptian hieroglyphics, he reasoned, maybe there was a language somewhere that could help unlock the mysterious phrases that rang repeatedly from the tongues of his grandmother and her sisters during the long summers of his childhood in Tennessee. The man known as Kintay, the guitar-like instrument they called a ko, the lost river Kamby Bolongo—maybe these were not trapped in the past after all.

Could he somehow, somewhere, find a way to make the words of his ancestors speak again? And did the secret lay further away, further back in time, than he had ever before let himself imagine—beyond Tennessee, beyond colonial Virginia, and back to the African homeland of his distant ancestors? To tell the story of Will and Cynthia Palmer, their daughter Bertha, son-in-law Simon, and their restless, precocious grandson Alex, would he also have to tell the story of Kintay, the man his grandmother and her sisters called the African?

The thought disturbed and captivated Haley as he left the museum and made plans to return to the United States. "My plane from London was circling to land at New York," he later recalled, "with me wondering: What specific African tongue was it? Was there any way in the world that maybe I could find out?"

A year earlier, in August 1964, Haley and his literary agent, Paul Reynolds, had first met with Kenneth McCormick, a senior editor at Doubleday, and his assistant, Lisa Drew. The group's topic for discussion at lunch that afternoon was Haley's still "rather nebulous idea" for a book-length account of

Haley's idea for a book about his family history found an enthusiastic audience in Doubleday editors Kenneth McCormick and Lisa Drew (right). "The whole thing was very exciting," remembered Drew years later. "To my knowledge, no black writer had ever traced his origins back through slavery."

the gripping family history he had learned as a child in Tennessee.

McCormick and Drew were immediately impressed, both by the novelty of Haley's idea and the enthusiasm he brought to the project. "The whole thing was very exciting," recalled Drew more than 25 years after her first encounter with Haley. "To my knowledge, no black writer had ever traced his origins back through slavery."

Following the meeting, Doubleday signed Haley to write a book about his family's triumph over slavery, advancing him $5,000 to cover his expenses researching and writing the book. The outline for the story was already there, Haley insisted, in his memories of his Grandma Palmer's front porch sermons.

But *Before This Anger*—as Haley was calling the project at the time—could not actually be written until he was able to finish the remaining archival research necessary to confirm and expand his grandmother's recollections. Such research would, of course, take time: several months in addition to the extensive work that he already done. And it would also take money. At the time of Haley's meeting with the editors from Doubleday, $5,000 seemed a generous sum, more than adequate to cover the cost of the project. But that was all about to change.

Hardly a year later, mistakenly thinking that the research for the book was already nearing completion, Haley retreated to his home/studio in Rome, New York, where he had written the bulk of *The Autobiography of Malcolm X* the previous year and where he now felt confident he could begin to pull together his new book. "I write better there than anywhere else," he confided to an interviewer in 1966 not long after starting to write. "It's a very hospitable town. And the Jarvis Library is one of the finest small libraries I've seen anywhere."

At the time, Haley was in fact so confident that he would soon be finished with the book that he was already outlining the plans for a number of other articles and a somewhat surprising excursion into the theater. "I have material for a musical comedy that I want to do," he told the same interviewer.

But there were to be no musical comedies on Alex Haley's horizon in the years that followed. The family saga for which he had contracted to Doubleday quickly began to get out of hand. "It soon became apparent," Drew remembered, "that the book was evolving into a much bigger project than he had originally conceived." With each of his unexpected appearances at the Doubleday offices, Haley brought some intriguing new discovery that promised both to enrich the contents of the book and further delay the date of its completion.

"Alex would occasionally pop into town without giving us any notice," Drew recalled of the series of sudden, dramatic transitions that would characterize the evolution of the project and her own relationship with Haley. "Ken was never able to make lunch on

After days of travel on the Gambia River, Haley finally arrived at the dusty little village of Juffure. The author was shocked to discover that the village's 70 inhabitants lived much the way his ancestor Kunta Kinte might have lived 200 years earlier—in round mud houses with dirt floors and pointed thatch roofs.

such short notice, and of course I could." The sessions between Haley and his editors soon became less and less frequent and the manuscript further and further behind schedule.

As he had expected, Haley had little problem finding the records he needed in the United States. Everywhere he went to do research—the U.S. Archives, the Library of Congress, numerous state and local archives, the DAR Library—the details of Cynthia Palmer's story proved remarkably accurate. "It was . . . uncanny," he later confessed of his own amazement at finally seeing his grandmother's memory confirmed in black and white, "staring at those names actually right there in official U.S. Government records."

The officially documented account of the story soon began to unfold before his eyes, just as he had heard it as a child. Kizzy, Chicken George, Tom—they were all there, right where they were supposed to be. But one very special element was still missing. As far as his official research was concerned, the story still lacked a beginning. How did his people actually make their way to this country? And where and how did they live before they came here?

In Gambia, Haley learned of the griots, very old men who had memorized the entire oral histories of their clans and would recite them in trancelike states on special occasions in their villages. It was rumored that some of the griots could talk about African history for as long as three whole days without repeating themselves.

To know that, of course, he would have to go to Africa. But Africa was a huge continent, with many different cultures and many different languages, and Haley had no idea where to begin looking for his past.

Out of desperation, Haley began to haunt the entranceway to the United Nations headquarters in New York. He could easily recognize the African delegates by their jet-black skin, a trick he had learned from Malcolm X, and he would stop many of them as they were leaving for the day and ask if they could identify any of the words he had learned from his grandmother. Everyone to whom he talked seemed interested in his work and sympathetic to his predicament, but no one could recognize the strange language he was doing his best to speak.

Finally, just when it was beginning to seem he would never be able to trace his family back to Africa, Haley learned from a friend that Dr. Jan Vansina, a very knowledgeable African linguist at the University of Wisconsin, might be able to help him. Arriving at Dr. Vansina's home in Wisconsin the very next day, Haley learned that the words were probably Mandinkan, the language spoken by the Mandingo people in Gambia.

In Gambia not long afterward, Haley was able to confirm Dr. Vansina's suspicions about the origin of his grandmother's mysterious language. The Kamby Bolongoa, he was told, was the Mandingo name for the Gambia River; a ko was probably a "kora," a traditional African instrument resembling a guitar; and the name Kintay—or Kinte, as he learned it was spelled—belonged to a highly revered family in Mandingo history. In fact, the lengthy, hyphenated names of several Gambian villages contained the word Kinte, designating that a member of the Kinte family had either founded them or played some significant role in their development.

While he was in Gambia, Haley also learned about the old men called griots, who could still be found in the country's most isolated regions. Routinely trained for a period of 40 to 50 years, griots were the oral historians of the Mandingo people and were virtual walking genealogies. Through these men, each village was able to preserve its own history: the story of its founding; the records of marriages, births, and deaths; and tales of extraordinary individuals. Many of the griots, Haley was told, could recite their story for as long as three days without once repeating themselves.

Upon his return to the United States, Haley began to reflect on the significance of what he had learned. With their joyful, insistent gossiping about their pasts—he was slowly beginning to realize—his grandmother and her sisters had, in a very real sense, served as griots for the Palmer clan, preserving in their memory the American half of the story line that had been broken when his ancestor, Kinte, was stolen from his home almost 200 years earlier. Somewhere, perhaps, there was an African griot who could help him put the two stories together again. But where? Haley still did not know the answer when he returned from Africa.

Within a few weeks, Haley received a registered letter from Gambia. He was thrilled to learn that a griot had been located who might be able to help him. By now, however, the $5,000 from Doubleday was long gone, and Haley simply did not have the money to return to Africa.

Broke and desperate, but determined somehow to make the trip, Haley approached the owners of *Reader's Digest*, Lila and DeWitt Wallace. Years earlier, when he was just beginning his career as a writer, Lila Wallace had told Haley to call on her if he ever needed help. If there ever was to be such a time, Haley reasoned, this was it. He explained his situation to the wealthy publisher, and shortly after his visit he received a letter informing him that *Reader's Digest* would provide him with $300 a month for a year in addition to any "reasonable necessary travel expenses" related to his current project.

Haley left for Africa as soon as he could book a flight. Upon his return to Gambia, he was shocked to learn that he would have to organize his own safari to reach the griot's village, a settlement called Juffure, far up the Gambia River. Finally, after what seemed like endless days of preparation and travel, he and his entourage arrived at the tiny village.

Haley was completely unprepared for what he found there. Without as much as a word, the villagers immediately began to surround him, staring intensely at his face and his clothing. "A kind of visceral

A Return of the Shipping arrived at and sailed from James Fort Gambia Commm: *May 5 1767*

After days of sifting through endless files of ship logs at Lloyds of London, Haley discovered that a British slave ship, the Lord Ligonier, *had sailed from the Gambia River to Annapolis, Maryland, on July 5, 1767— the same period of time that, according to the griot in Juffure, "the King's soldiers" arrived in Africa.*

surging or a churning sensation started up deep inside me," he later remembered. "Bewildered, I was won-dering what on earth was this . . . then in a little while it was rather as if some force of realization rolled in on me: Many times in my life I had been among crowds of people, but never where every one was jet black!" Unbeknownst to Haley at the time, the villagers, none of whom had ever before seen a black American, were having a similarly disorient-ing experience.

Suddenly, the griot appeared among the crowd. He was a small, intense man dressed in a traditional white robe and wearing a tight pillbox hat. After the two men had been introduced by the interpreters and Haley's business there had been explained, the griot sat on the ground in front of his guest and began to speak slowly but deliberately, in an eerie, trance-like state.

Sitting quietly among the villagers, Haley heard what seemed like an endless list of tribal births, marriages, and deaths in the Kinte family. Remem-bering he had heard that griots sometimes recited up to three days at a time, he began to fear that he might

CHARLES WALLACE.

Annapolis, Sept. 29, 1767.

JUST IMPORTED,

In the Ship LORD LIGONIER, *Capt.* DAVIES, *from the River* GAMBIA, *in* AFRICA, *and to be sold by the Subscribers, in* ANNAPOLIS, *for Cash, or good Bills of Exchange, on Wednesday the* 7*th of* October *next,*

A CARGO of CHOICE HEALTHY SLAVES. The said Ship will take TOBACCO to LONDON, on Liberty, at 6*l.* Sterling per Ton.

JOHN RIDOUT,
DANIEL OF ST. THO*s*. JENIFER.

N. B. Any Person that will contract for a Quantity of Lumber, may meet with Encouragement, by applying to D. T. JENIFER.

"Just Imported, in the ship Lord Ligonier . . . a cargo of choice healthy slaves." Back in the United States, Haley discovered this tiny entry from the Maryland Gazette *on a microfilm roll in the Maryland Hall of Records in Annapolis. Haley had finally found the time and the place that his ancestors had first arrived in America.*

never hear the information he was seeking. Then, two hours into his presentation, the griot began to tell the tale of a man named Omoro Kinte who had four sons. "About the time the King's soldiers came," the old man recited as Haley suddenly caught his breath, "the oldest of these sons, Kunta, went away from his village to chop wood . . . and he was never seen again."

Haley later described the griot's revelation as the most powerful moment of his life. "I sat as if I were carved of stone," he remembered of his initial response to the story of Kunta Kinte. "My blood seemed to have congealed. This man whose lifetime had been in this back-country African village had no way in the world to know that he had just echoed what I had heard all through my boyhood years on my grandma's front porch in Henning, Tennessee . . . of an African who always had insisted that his name was 'Kin-tay'; who had called a guitar a 'ko,' and a river within the state of Virginia, 'Kamby Bolongo'; and who had been kidnapped into slavery while not far from his village, chopping wood, to make himself a drum."

Throughout his childhood, Haley's grandmother had insisted that a ship had first brought the African to a place called 'Naples. Reasoning that 'Naples had to have been Annapolis, Maryland, and that the "King's soldiers" mentioned by the griot belonged to the British military, Haley soon flew to London to discover which, if any, British slave ships had sailed from the Gambia River to Annapolis during the 1760s.

After more than six weeks of painstaking research, poring through hundreds of slave-ship records from the period, Haley finally had his answer. Only one such ship had sailed that particular route during those years: a vessel known as the *Lord Ligonier* had departed the waters of the Gambia River on July 5, 1767, on its way to the auction block in Annapolis.

The next afternoon, Haley was back in the United States, crouched dutifully at a desk in the Maryland Hall of Records. Sifting through endless microfilm rolls of the old *Maryland Gazette* for the year 1767, his tired eyes came across an advertisement in the October 1 edition: "JUST IMPORTED, In the ship Lord Ligonier, Capt. Davies, from the River Gambia, in Africa, and to be sold by the subscribers, in Annapolis, for cash, or good bills of exchange on Wednesday the 7th of October next, A Cargo of CHOICE HEALTHY SLAVES."

As quickly as he had arrived in Annapolis, Haley went to Richmond, Virginia, where he plunged frantically into the filmed records of legal deeds for the years following 1767 in Spotsylvania County, the region where his grandmother had claimed the African had first been enslaved. On a deed dated September 5, 1768, he found a lengthy account of a transfer of property from John Waller to his brother William Waller. Among the goods exchanged was listed "a Negro man slave named Toby." 🔊

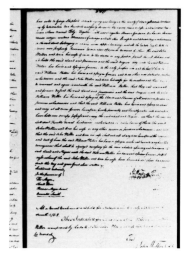

In Richmond, Virginia, the author discovered an old deed in which the ownership of a "Negro man slave named Toby" had been transferred by John Waller to his brother William. "In the twelve years since my visit to the Rosetta Stone," Haley later reflected on his feelings at the time, "I have traveled half a million miles, I suppose, searching, sifting, checking, crosschecking, finding out more and more about the people whose respective oral histories had proved not only to be correct, but even to connect on both sides of the ocean."

6

AN AMERICAN SAGA

As ALEX HALEY continued to work on the book about his family, the normally skeptical writer could never quite shake the memory of a conversation he had had with his cousin Georgia in 1966. At the time, she was the sole survivor among the group of women from whom he had first learned of his African ancestry.

Haley had visited the old woman shortly before she died, to share the news that he had finally been able to document in writing "at least the highlights of the cherished family story." To the author's bewilderment, the aging matriarch had not seemed in the least surprised, either by the startling accuracy of the stories she had told, or the strange series of "coincidences" that had enabled her grandnephew to confirm them. This was a story that the ancestors wanted to be told, she reminded him. They had, in fact, chosen him to tell it. He must never forget, she cautioned, that Kintay, Kizzy, Chicken George, Tom, his grandmother Cynthia—all of them were "up there watchin'" him, and they would make sure that he got it right.

If, as Haley began to suspect, his forefathers and mothers were somehow guiding him to the informa-

Following on the remarkable success of the book, the miniseries "Roots: The Triumph of an American Family" was the costliest and most lavish production in the history of television. By the time Chicken George led the family to freedom in the series' final episode, more than 90 million Americans sat glued to their television sets—the largest single audience ever.

tion for the book, they grew strangely silent when the time came actually to begin writing.

As a result of his successful research, the story of Haley's childhood memories of his grandmother's tales of her family and their rise from slavery had now become the great saga of Kunta Kinte, from his enslavement in Africa to the eventual prosperity and triumph of his ancestors in the New World. And what had once been a modestly conceived memoir about his childhood in Tennessee had now expanded to epic proportions. Even if he could find all the information he needed, how in the world would he ever find the time and the energy to finish the book he now envisioned?

But the biggest problem Haley now faced was that there was simply no written history about most of the events and experiences that he planned to describe. The day-to-day routine of village life in 18th-century Africa, the agony of life aboard a slave ship, the problems facing blacks in colonial America—these were all things that Haley would have to find for himself. He now set out on a seemingly endless period of research and travel, checking and cross-checking records in libraries, archives, museums, and villages around the world. By the time the project was completed, Haley would later brag, he had talked with thousands and thousands of people, studied untold numbers of records, and visited more than 50 libraries and archives on three continents.

Easily the most agonizing bit of research involved the initial enslavement of the boy Kunta Kinte and his perilous journey across the Atlantic Ocean aboard the slave ship, the *Lord Ligonier*. Not satisfied with his own extensive experiences at sea in the Coast Guard, Haley decided that if he was to portray effectively the terrors confronting his protagonist, he would first have to subject himself to at least some of

Although Haley retired from the Coast Guard at the age of 37, he never lost his passion for the sea. Haley often bragged that most of Roots was written aboard ship, apart from the pressures of deadlines and speaking engagements. Throughout his later years, the author and his childhood buddy George Sims would hop aboard the nearest steamer whenever Haley's schedule would allow.

the discomforts that young Kinte must have endured during the crossing.

With this in mind, Haley flew once again to Africa, eventually locating a freighter, called the *African Star*, whose regular route was similar to that crossed by the *Lord Ligonier* two centuries earlier. Securing a place on board, he made special arrangements with the ship's captain to simulate the conditions he had learned were involved in an actual slave crossing. "After each late evening's dinner," Haley later described, "I climbed down successive metal ladders into [the ship's] deep, dark, cold cargo hold. Stripping to my underwear, I lay on my back on a wide rough bare dunnage plank and forced myself to stay there through all ten nights of the crossing, trying to imagine what did he see, hear, feel, smell, taste—and above all, in knowing Kunta, what things did he think?"

Haley's 10-day crossing could offer only the slightest hint of the real agonies faced by real slaves; during the 80 to 90 days they were imprisoned at sea, they had to withstand much harsher conditions. The experience was more than enough, however, to have a profound impact on the author, eliminating any lingering doubts he might have had about finishing the project.

"That was the hardest part," he later confessed to an interviewer, "writing about the slave ship. There were times on that boat I felt like jumping off. I was deep in debt by then, felt I'd never finish the damn book. One time I must have been almost mad with despair, because I went into a sort of dream, and I really thought I heard the dead voices of my family talking to me, encouraging me. That was what kept me going in the end. After that I felt I really had to do it, for them."

Haley found that life at sea did have one real advantage, however. For once, he was able to avoid the pressures and deadlines he faced at home and concentrate simply on the task at hand. Along with his main researcher and childhood friend George Sims, the harried writer would continue to sneak away on the first available cargo ship whenever he had the chance, often for as long as two months at a

The poet Maya Angelou (pictured here with Haley and actor Levar Burton) was one of the many distinguished African-Americans who lent their presence to the "Roots" television project. The program featured the largest, most gifted cast of black actors that the American public had ever beheld.

time. It was frequently the only time he could manage to get any real writing done.

"The quiet allows you to get to be one with whatever you're working on," he explained years later to an interviewer about his ongoing passion for life and work at sea. By the time the manuscript was finally completed, Haley reported, he had spent the vast majority of time actually writing it in seclusion, aboard one of his beloved cargo ships or at an equally remote island retreat in Jamaica.

The most distressing deadline, of course, was the one Haley faced at Doubleday, where Ken Mc-Cormick and Lisa Drew were understandably beginning to wonder if they would ever see a finished manuscript. "I can't remember when we first received the actual copy," Drew confessed years later, "but I know that it was a long time coming, with longer and longer periods between our sessions with Alex."

By the time Haley delivered Doubleday the final book early in February 1976, it was almost 10 years past its original due date, his advance from Doubleday in travel and research expenses having swollen from $5,000 to $96,000. Even then, he was reluctant to let it go.

"They sent me my last draft for what was meant to be a final read-through," he laughed to a reporter a few months later about his by-then legendary difficulty making deadlines. The final editing was supposed to be a mere formality, taking no more than a couple of days. Faced, however, with the prospect of finally ending the project, Haley had second thoughts.

"I hid out in the Hotel Commodore so that Doubleday wouldn't know where I was," he continued, "and I did a whole new chapter and a lot of rewriting. It took me two weeks, and for the last 48 hours I worked around the clock. Then I sent it off by messenger, and got on a plane for Indiana, where

With his quick wit and insistent humor, stage actor Ben Vereen turned Haley's great-grandfather Chicken George into the favorite character of most viewers. Many viewers—and actors—however, were affected by the darker side of the story. During filming, one of the black actors in the slave-ship sequence was so moved by his role that he angrily hurled the white actor playing the shipmaster overboard.

I was supposed to give a lecture, and the next thing I remember is when I woke up there, knowing it was all over."

By the time that *Roots: The Saga of an American Family* finally began to appear on the shelves of bookstores in September 1976, it represented one of the most eagerly awaited publications in the history of American literature. No one was disappointed. In an early promotional blurb, James Baldwin, Haley's longtime friend and mentor from his early days as a starving young writer in Greenwich Village, referred to the book as "an act of love, faith and courage." And an early review in the *New York Times* correctly anticipated the book's broad appeal beyond racial lines, declaring to the paper's millions of readers that Haley "speaks not only for America's black people, but for all of us everywhere."

Readers across the country agreed. *Roots* became the nation's best-selling book within a month of its September 17 publication date, with sales totaling more than half a million copies by the end of the year. And in addition to the book's enormous success, negotiations were already under way between Doubleday and the ABC television network for a $6 million, 12-hour miniseries based on Haley's work. For his part in the combined projects, Haley asked for and was promptly rewarded with the monumental sum of $1 million. It would quickly turn out to be a bargain for both ABC and Doubleday.

After years and years of living hand-to-mouth, Haley had at last become a millionaire, just as he had predicted to his pal C. Eric Lincoln more than 20 years earlier. Shortly before the book was published, the now-celebrated author talked openly about the probable impact that his sudden wealth would have on his future writing projects.

"I had always wondered what a million-dollar author was like," he confessed. "Now I've met two of them, Arthur Hailey and Harold Robbins, and it seems I'll be one myself. I shan't exactly make whoopee with the money," he added somewhat apologetically. "It just means I'll have the funds to finance the travel and research for the writing I want to do. And in the future I'd like not to have advances any more. If they're small, they're not enough, and then if you get a track record, they're too big, and that pressures you. The main thing is to be free, and that's something I've always wanted to be."

Six months later, Haley's life-style had changed very little. About the only things the once-impoverished writer had bought for himself were a stereo, a television, and a brand-new videotape player on which "to watch reruns of the [forthcoming] series." The most substantial change, according to Haley, was the reduction in stress he felt in knowing for the first time in his career as a writer that he would be able to pay his monthly bills. "It really startles me that the last thing I think of now is money," he shared with one reporter.

The immediate success of *Roots* was no accident, however. Haley had worked long and hard to make sure that his book got the public exposure and critical attention he felt that it deserved. For almost 10 years, he balanced the time he spent researching and writing the book with what eventually became a breathless schedule of interviews, lectures, and public appearances around the country. During the six years leading up to the publication alone, Haley once bragged to an interviewer, he estimated that he must have talked to more than a million people. "If they all buy a copy," he joked prophetically at the time, "we're in."

Even before Haley had completed the book, a scramble among the networks for the rights to Haley's historical drama set the Hollywood rumor mills in a flurry that Haley would later describe as "even yakkier than the publishing one," giving even more free

In one of the series' most moving scenes, actor James Earl Jones portrays the moment when Haley first made the acquaintance of his ancestors in the village of Juffure. "They hadn't been looking at me as an individual," Haley would later explain why all the villagers had reached out to touch him. "I represented in their eyes a symbol of the twenty-five millions of us black people whom they had never seen, who lived beyond an ocean."

publicity to the *Roots* phenomenon. But no one anywhere was quite prepared for what was about to happen next.

"Roots: The Triumph of an American Family" began airing on ABC right in the middle of the networks' ratings wars. Costing $6 million to produce, the most for any television production in history at the time, the 12-hour, six-night miniseries portrayed the Haley saga all the way from the childhood and enslavement of Kunta Kinte in Gambia to the dramatic conclusion in which Chicken George led his family to freedom in Tennessee.

The program featured the largest, most gifted cast of black actors that the American public had ever beheld, as well as the first extended dramatic presentation of black family life in this country in the history of network television. It proved to be a powerful experience for everyone involved in the production. In fact, one of the young black actors in the slave-ship sequence was so moved by his role, Haley incredulously reported to an interviewer at the time, that he angrily hurled the white actor playing the shipmaster overboard.

And just as Haley's long-winded, virtually unedited interviews for *Playboy* had transformed the acceptable format for magazine interviews almost 15 years earlier, the "Roots" series was about to change the way Americans watched television. Breaking the proven formula for running a miniseries in consecutive weekly installments that ABC had established with its enormously popular "Rich Man, Poor Man" series the year before, the network chose instead to run "Roots" on successive nights. "If it turned out to be a gigantic flop," reasoned reviewer Richard Levine with cynical hindsight, "it would at least be a self-contained flop."

"Roots" was anything but a flop. By the time Chicken George led the family to freedom in the

Haley first learned that he had been awarded a special Pulitzer Prize for Roots *in the company of his two younger brothers, Julius, a navy architect, and George, a Washington bureaucrat. Though the award was swamped by controversy from the beginning, it would remain the proudest achievement of the author's career.*

series' final episode, more than 90 million Americans sat glued to their television sets, the largest single audience in television history. The series was so successful, in fact, that at the time all six of its episodes were rated among the 13 most-watched television shows of all time.

The following year, ABC produced and aired a sequel, offering television viewers the rest of Haley's story. "Roots: The Next Generation" featured an even larger and more distinguished cast than the series' first installment, including James Earl Jones portraying the author as he searched across three continents for his lost family history, and Marlon Brando as the American Nazi leader George Lincoln Rockwell, whom Haley had interviewed for *Playboy*.

To the author's delight, the network recreated an exact, life-size replica of his childhood home in Henning, Tennessee, for the shooting, including the Palmer estate and his grandfather's lumber company. Less to his liking, though, were some of the liberties that the director and writers took with the facts and events that it had taken him so long to get right. In one particularly glaring scene, Haley's grandfather

Will Palmer held the infant Alex to the starlit sky in the same mysterious ritual with which Kunta Kinte named his daughter Kizzy several generations earlier, giving viewers the mistaken impression that it was grandfather Will, and not his wife Cynthia, who was heir to the Kinte legend. But the public loved it, and by now well more than half the people in America had seen at least a part of the *Roots* saga portrayed on television.

In a little over a year, Haley had become one of the best-known and most highly celebrated writers in the world. Sales on the book then totaled more than 8 million copies worldwide, with versions available in 31 different languages. A Roper poll conducted during the period found Haley to be the third most admired black man in America, behind heavyweight champion Muhammad Ali and entertainer Stevie Wonder.

And the popular success of the book was equalled by its critical reception. By his own calculation, Haley would receive almost 300 awards, special citations, or honorary degrees for his work on *Roots*. The greatest honor of all came in April 1977, when the 56-year-old author was awarded a special Pulitzer Prize, the most prestigious American literary award, for his ground-breaking epic. In presenting Haley with the award, the Pulitzer Committee cited Haley's "important contribution to the history of slavery." Receiving the prize would remain the most cherished honor in Haley's highly celebrated career as an author.

But Haley was about to discover that fame and wealth could have their dark side as well. Rather than providing him with the creative freedom for which he had worked so long and so stubbornly, the unprecedented popularity of *Roots* was about to bring his writing career to a grinding halt. ❧

7

BACKLASH

❧

THINGS BEGAN TO take an ominous turn for Alex Haley early in 1977, even before the celebrated writer had found time to enjoy his newly found celebrity.

For one thing, the 56-year-old author was simply worn out. All the years of nonstop research, writing, and public appearances—during which the indefatigable Haley often worked 15 to 16 hours a day, seven days a week—had finally begun to take their toll. At the beginning of February, a combination of physical exhaustion and a light case of pneumonia sent him to bed for several weeks, forcing him to cancel an extended series of speaking engagements around the country. It was the first time in almost 20 years that the normally tireless writer had been forced to slow down.

The always restless Haley was soon back on his feet, however, and wondering out loud to friends and reporters about what his next project would be. But even before he had a chance to get started, his career was stalled once again. A flood of court cases and public accusations threatened to destroy the success and public recognition that he had worked so hard to achieve.

Because of the enormous success of Roots, *Haley found little time for office work—or for writing—in the years that followed. Most of his time was spent on the road, where he would regularly speak at campuses, community group meetings, and conventions, 150 or more during a single year. Pictured here with his longtime secretary, Jackie Naipo, the author takes a rare opportunity to check his mail.*

Oddly enough, it was Haley himself who filed the first of the several legal complaints in which his life would soon become entangled. On March 16, 1977, the author, along with the Kinte Corporation, the organization he had founded for the purpose of investing his profits from *Roots*, filed suit against Doubleday for punitive damages of $5 million for five instances of breach of contract.

The charges centered around what Haley believed at the time to be the publishing company's failure to market the best-selling book in a way that insured that his best interests were protected. Haley had long maintained that it was because of his ongoing lectures, interviews, and other public appearances that *Roots* had so quickly become a bestseller, and not because of the promotional efforts of the publisher. In addition, as he told the court at the time, it was he, and not his publishers, who had negotiated the deal with ABC that had resulted in the popular miniseries.

The negotiations and tireless self-promotion were things that Haley could otherwise have lived with; he had, in fact, described them proudly and humorously to numerous interviewers in the months preceding the suit. What really distressed Haley was Doubleday's decision to bring out a paperback version of the book at a time when he felt it would threaten additional sales of the still-profitable hardcover edition. This move, and the company's failure to print enough copies to cover the enormous demand following the airing of the television series, were largely responsible for his decision to take his publishers to court.

Less than a month later, Doubleday publicly rejected Haley's accusations, asserting that it was the author, with his repeated inability to meet his deadlines for the book, who had violated the terms of his contract. Despite the inflammatory language used by both sides in the disagreement, the case was concerned strictly with the best way to market the book and did not jeopardize Haley's long-term relationship with his editors. "There is no animosity between Haley and ourselves," reported Doubleday's general counsel James McGreath at the time. "We protect all our authors just as we protect ourselves, and we will fight just as hard for Haley in this matter as we will fight for ourselves."

The dispute would prove to be academic in the end. In spite of the ongoing disagreement, the book continued to sell at a record pace.

More unsettling developments quickly followed, however. New stories began to break that challenged the factual basis of Haley's ground-breaking "historical novel." Haley had, in fact, anticipated the skepticism that many readers might bring to a work of history for which few—or in some cases, no—known written resources were available. "I call it 'faction,'" he explained to one interviewer shortly after the book was published. "All the major incidents are true, the details are as accurate as very heavy research can make them, the names and dates are real, but obviously when it comes to dialogue, and people's emotions and thoughts, I had to make things up."

The issue was first raised at the time that Haley was awarded the Pulitzer Prize. The Pulitzer Committee had acknowledged their own problems with some of the historical content of Haley's story by awarding him with a "special" prize, rather than an award in the category of history. Haley's work, the committee insisted at the time, "did not accommodate itself to the category of history but transcended it."

In a biting editorial, Mark O'Haway of London's *Sunday Times* sharply disagreed, questioning both the accuracy of Haley's account and the integrity of his research. The Pulitzer Committee stood by its original decision, however, stating that, "regardless

Among those who flocked to hear Haley speak wherever he went were thousands of African-Americans, for whom Haley's personal saga was a source of inspiration and pride. "Because of Roots," *he later wrote proudly, "many blacks have said that Kunta Kinte, my forebear, has become their ancestor."*

of error, the historical essence of [Haley's] book was truthful."

Even more disturbing were the public accusations by two highly respected black novelists that Haley had improperly used parts of their published work in writing *Roots*. The first and angrier of the charges came from Mississippi novelist Margaret Walker, author of the award-winning novel *Jubilee*. In April 1977, Walker sued Haley and Doubleday, claiming that large sections of her novel of life on a 19th-century Georgia plantation were stolen by Haley.

Walker offered the court no direct evidence of specific passages she felt had been plagiarized, claiming that the similarities were too numerous to mention. A district court judge ruled that her charges were completely ungrounded and quickly dismissed the case. But Haley wound up paying more than $100,000 in legal fees, and Walker would continue to make public accusations against Haley in the years that followed.

Almost simultaneously, a more troubling case emerged. Harold Courlander, author of *The African*, publicly accused Haley of using more than 80 specific passages from his novel in developing the African sections of *Roots*. "Certain thoughts of Kunta Kinte, certain scenes and dialogues, certain concepts and certain imagery in *Roots* do seem quite similar to various moments in *The African*," Courlander said in a statement issued to the *New York Times* only two days after Walker had filed her suit.

After carefully weighing Courlander's charges to the press, representatives from Doubleday felt strongly that there was insufficient evidence to justify a verdict of copyright infringement. The similarities between the two books, they maintained, were the inevitable result of the common limited resources that both men were forced to use in preparing their books, such as shared folklore and the few available slave ship records. "Whenever there is a tidal wave of good reaction to a book," explained Haley's editor Ken McCormick, "a writer who has written on the same subject innocently relates himself to it. There were only a limited number of possibilities that a black could have experienced during the period dealt with, and there are bound to be similarities."

Haley, however, conducted his own private investigation, discovering to his horror that three direct, almost verbatim passages from *The African* had in fact somehow found their way into his book. He explained to his fellow author that, throughout his years of research, friends and acquaintances would often present him with scattered notes and unattributed information. The sources for most were tracked and properly documented or else not used directly in the manuscript. Apparently, portions of Courlander's novel had somehow slipped through this screening process and had thus ended up in the final draft of *Roots*.

Haley presented the author of *The African* with an out-of-court settlement of $500,000, against the counsel of Doubleday. "We didn't believe he should have settled," remembered Lisa Drew. "It seemed to us he could have paid a personal permission fee." But Haley felt differently. In making the settlement, he insisted at the time, he hoped both to make reparations to Courlander and to protect the integrity of his own work. "*Roots*," he told one reporter after the controversy had finally subsided, "is one of the major symbols of hope and pride for a whole people and I didn't want to see it get scarred by implication and innuendo."

Although rumors of plagiarism and fabrication in the writing of *Roots* would circulate for years, the settlement with Courlander represented a quick, if costly, end to the public part of the controversy. For Haley, however, the damage had already been done. He had spent the major part of his career researching and documenting *Roots*, and the accusations that someone else was responsible for his work broke his heart. "I think it hurt him personally deeply," Lisa Drew reflected a number of years later. "I'm not sure in a way that he ever entirely got over it."

Certainly, Haley would never fully recover his ambitions as a writer. "A whole lot of the thrill of writing books has been taken away from me by this experience," he confessed a couple of years after the settlement with Courlander. "I'd rather go into something where I can be more freely creative."

The stories would continue, however. To some, Haley's settlement with Courlander was an admission of guilt on a much broader scale, and Haley found himself dogged for years by questions about the controversy and rumors of other writers who claimed that they were really responsible for *Roots*. "For years afterward," Lisa Drew remembered, "people would ask, 'What about that plagiarism?'"

As things turned out, it was not the *Roots* scandal that would keep Haley's writing ambitions on hold during the years to follow but the book's continuing success. Within months, the still-energetic author forgot his vow to quit writing and began to talk openly about future projects.

But as more and more people read Haley's book or saw the television series, more and more invitations came from groups who wished to meet personally the man whose work had so affected their lives, and to hear firsthand the author's story of how the great book came to be written. Requests poured in from as far away as Africa, Latin America, and the

Surprisingly, Haley (pictured here with talk-show host Phil Donahue) also became a favorite with many white audiences. "You have given me a new awareness of your heritage," wrote one woman from California. "The people of Africa came alive and with them their beauty, pride, tradition and strength. Kunta Kinte is now a part of me. I will carry him, his family and his country with me and, hopefully, this new awareness will make me a better human being."

In spite of all the controversy surrounding Haley, the Roots *phenomenon continued throughout the world in the years that followed. By the end of the decade, the book had sold more than 8 million copies worldwide, with versions available in 31 different languages.*

former Soviet Union, where Haley would be featured at a Moscow University seminar on *Roots* and other important books by U.S. authors.

Haley's increasing popularity with the public did little to counter the unflattering press coverage that he still occasionally received. Probably the most unsettling news item for Haley was released in April 1980, following his long-awaited trip back to the village of Juffure in Gambia, where the author had first learned about his now-famous ancestor Kunta Kinte almost 15 years earlier.

Reacquainting himself with the villagers, Haley asked if there was anything he could do to repay the kindness and hospitality that they had shown to him on his first visit to Gambia. It was soon decided that he would provide the money to build the Muslim village a mosque. Before leaving, Haley gave a local contractor a check in the amount of $6,000 to begin the work. Haley intended to provide the additional cost of $18,000 as the work progressed.

A year later, the *Baltimore Sun* informed its readers that the proposed mosque had never been completed, with only a cinder-block shell standing unattended on the site. According to the elderly village chief, Bakaryding Taal, Haley "made a lot of promises, but has not done anything. My people are not angry," Taal insisted, "just disappointed."

Tracking down the contractor he had hired in Gambia, Haley learned that the mosque would in fact be built in due time, but that "everything moves so slowly in Africa." Haley did what he could to speed things up but could not hide his own disappointment, both with the press, which seemed eager to print anything bad about him it could find, and in the villagers of Juffure, who were perhaps expressing their frustration that the success of *Roots* had not done more to bring tourists and money to their homeland. "I'm not bitter," Haley said sadly at the time, "but I feel a bit wounded. I get a wonderful reception elsewhere in Africa."

4E 71

ALEX HALEY'S BOYHOOD HOME

Will Palmer, a prominent Henning businessman,
built this house in 1918-19. Palmer's grandson
Alex Haley lived here from 1921 to 1929 and
later spent many summers with his grandparents.
It was on the porch that he heard the stories
told by his grandmother and ⎯⎯ ⎯ ⎯ ⎯⎯ ⎯
inspired him to write his ⎯⎯ ⎯
rize-winning book Roo⎯
mericans watched
elevision adaptation.
ear

8

BACK TO TENNESSEE

••••••

THE 1980s BEGAN with Alex Haley wondering what to do next. Over time, his resolution never to write again had given way to his enthusiasm over a number of new projects: a children's novel; the memoirs of his childhood in Henning; and a longer, more substantive treatment of how *Roots* came to be written. But try as he might, he just did not seem to be getting anywhere with any of his ideas.

One major obstacle, understandably, was exhaustion. Since his brief illness and recuperation in 1977, Haley had resumed his frantic schedule of public appearances. Though he was now more than 60 years old, the widely celebrated author would often speak to more than 100 groups during the course of a year, sometimes traveling halfway across the world for a single appearance. This left little time, or energy, for research or writing.

"I just think he was too tired to do too much," reflected Haley's good friend A'Lelia Bundles, who first met the author in 1982, on his failure to get much writing done during his later years. "He was just too worn out." Even when Haley did have the energy to write, it was often difficult for him to actually find the time to spend in front of his typewriter.

Though he traveled all around the world in his later years, Alex Haley never lost his passion for his boyhood home of Henning, Tennessee. In the early 1980s, he purchased a large estate in neighboring Norris, Tennessee, just outside of Knoxville. And throughout most of the decade, he struggled to complete a novel based on the lives of the people he knew as a child.

During the 1980s, one of Haley's favorite pastimes was entertaining friends at his estate in Norris, Tennessee. The author is pictured here with a group of friends, including Maya Angelou (back row, fourth from left); Louis Gossett, Jr. (back row, right); and A'Lelia Bundles (front row, center), at one of these gatherings.

Despite Haley's hectic schedule of lectures and public appearances, he still managed to publish an occasional magazine article. The shortened version of the author's search for *Roots* finally appeared in the *Reader's Digest* in the late 1970s. In 1982, *Smithsonian* magazine published Haley's colorful account of the proud, strong-willed inhabitants of the South Carolina island community of Daufuskie and their struggle for survival in the face of the commercial development of their island. And throughout the 1980s, bits and pieces of the novel-in-progress *Henning*, the author's fictionalized account of his childhood in Tennessee, began to appear in print. In 1988, Haley even published a small book, a Christmas story entitled *A Different Kind of Christmas*.

But none of these works approached the kind of ambitious project that Haley still longed to tackle, something on the scale of *Roots* and *The Autobiography of Malcolm X*. His failure to do so was the one great disappointment of his later years. Embarrassed by his uncharacteristic lack of productivity, Haley would in the years that followed inform interviewer after interviewer that his next major work was nearing completion and would probably be out "by the end of the year." But though Haley could never fully accept it, that part of his life had ended with the publication of *Roots*. Neither *Henning* nor any of the author's other major projects would ever again find their way into print during his lifetime.

In many ways, as he would explain to one reporter more than 15 years after the publication of his most famous work, Haley was the victim of his own success. *Roots* and its depiction on television were so successful, Haley observed, "it's been just about near impossible for me to find the time to write the way I used to. For the last decade, I haven't been a writer. I've been the author of *Roots*, and I need to turn around. I've got to write."

Haley's first full-fledged attempt to reestablish himself as an important author was a proposed novel about the life of Madam C. J. Walker, America's first self-made millionairess. Haley initially turned his attention to the story of Madam Walker in 1982, when his childhood friend and researcher George Sims suggested that the legendary, turn-of-the-century cosmetics tycoon would be an interesting subject for Haley's next major project. "Madam played an amazing role in the advancement of blacks," Haley later explained to an interviewer concerning his interest in writing about a figure whose fame was not always associated with the advancement of her race, "much more than is commonly recognized."

Enlisting the assistance of Walker's great-great-granddaughter, A'Lelia Bundles, Haley began work on the project that same year. Bundles was a field producer with NBC News at the time and would soon become one of Haley's closest friends. By the following year, most of the research for the book had been completed and Haley was all set to begin writing. At the time, the always-optimistic Haley was already assuring interviewers that the book would be finished within a year or two.

Although Haley would continue to work on the Walker project for years, he soon became distracted from his writing when another, more personal ambition suddenly began to surface in his life. Up until this time, the notoriously restless author had spent much of his life on the go, trying to avoid the pressures and constraints of work and family life. But now for the first time, he found himself looking for a place to settle down, relax, and spend time with his friends.

In 1983, while on a visit to the Museum of Appalachia in Knoxville, Tennessee, Haley stumbled across an old Civil War plantation in neighboring Norris. The 127-acre estate came complete with an original white wood-framed farmhouse, guest quarters, and dark, rolling hills of scenic but unattended farmland.

When Haley first laid eyes on it, the once stately old farmhouse was slowly falling apart, with neither electricity nor running water, and the countryside was overgrown from years and years of neglect. But somehow Haley saw at once the home for which he had been searching, even if no one else shared his enthusiasm. Much of the property was in such disrepair, in fact, that Haley's closest friends were afraid that the overworked writer had "lost his cotton-pickin' mind," as he would later jokingly remind them, when he finally decided to purchase the large farm only a few months after discovering it. The estate would prove to be Haley's greatest source of pleasure throughout the next decade, as well as his most time-consuming, and finally heartbreaking, project.

"For years, I made considerable money from *Roots* and its byproducts," Haley explained of his seemingly impulsive decision to purchase the land. "But as I looked around, I discovered that I didn't own a thing in the world. So I got hold of this property and developed it. Now the joy is that I have a place where I can do what seems to me the biggest pleasure in the world—to get together with friends on weekends. Now I have something I can share with my friends."

Three years and hundreds of thousands of dollars later, Haley was finally ready to open his new home to colleagues and friends. The once dilapidated old farm had been transformed into one of the most spectacular estates in the South, complete with additional guest houses, retreat facilities, and an outdoor bandstand. The spacious, elegantly refurnished old farmhouse even included a museumlike display of the author's most cherished possessions, featuring his special Pulitzer Prize, the original manuscripts to *Roots* and *The Autobiography of Malcolm X*, and an actual ship's log from the *Lord Ligonier*, the same ship on which Kunta Kinte had sailed to America.

"I got to thinking," Haley said in describing to an interviewer the rationale for the estate's grand scale and elaborate facilities, "how nice it would be if there were just a place where I could say, 'Look, guys, let's figure out when we can all get a weekend off so you can come on down to my place.' This place is designed with that in mind."

Friendship was something for which Haley was never lacking. From his childhood days in Henning to his years on the road as a public speaker, the charming, down-to-earth writer was constantly forming enduring relationships wherever he went. It was sadly ironic, however, that an author who had achieved fame and fortune writing about the "triumph of an American family," as the "Roots" miniseries was aptly subtitled, should wish to spend his last years surrounded by his friends—but not his family. Yet it was consistent with the way he had lived his life for the past 40 years. Though Haley would never escape his nostalgia for the tight-knit, extended family of his early childhood in Henning, his own attempts to build a family always seemed to fall short.

After leaving his home to sail with the Coast Guard at the age of 17, Haley had married his first wife, Nannie Branch, only two years later. The marriage lasted 23 years in all and produced two children, but the couple rarely spent time together, either during Haley's 20 years at sea or the hectic early years of his literary apprenticeship in New York. They were divorced in 1964.

After Haley's second marriage, to Juliette Collins in 1964, also ended in divorce, he became involved with and married Myra Lewis, one of his researchers on the *Roots* project. Though the two would remain good friends, the marriage quickly deteriorated, with Lewis living and working in Los Angeles, while Haley spent most of the little time he was not at work on the road back home in Tennessee.

As Haley later explained to an interviewer, it was his own passion for writing that was responsible for the failure of each of his marriages. "In both cases, the 'other woman' was a typewriter," he reflected of his first two spouses' frequent complaint that he viewed them as less important than his work. "I couldn't deny it. If I could be cloned, I'd like to be three people. One would stay at the desk writing; one would be a public writer, the one who goes around making speeches and being personable; and the third would be a personal human being. A writer cannot be all these things at one time."

After the enormous success of *Roots*, Haley had inevitably chosen the life of the public writer, or had it chosen for him. Part of the problem was the

unusually personable author's lifelong inability to say no to anyone who asked him to speak or make an appearance. At the time, this was complicated by Haley's conviction that for many people *Roots* was much more than just another best-seller. As one woman would write him shortly after *Roots* was published, "This is not a book. This is my history."

It was a message and a responsibility that Haley took to heart. As the author of *Roots*, he understood that he embodied the struggle of millions of Americans, both black and white, to come to terms with their history and their identity. He felt that he owed his presence to those who wished to talk with him or hear him speak. "My reaction to the heroic status ascribed to *Roots*," he proclaimed in one article,

Pictured here with his son William and grandson William, Jr., Haley always regretted the way in which the demands of his career kept him apart from his family and friends. "If I could be cloned," he told one reporter toward the end of his life, "I'd like to be three people. One would stay at the desk writing; one would be a public writer, the one who goes around making speeches and being personable; and the third would be a personal human being. A writer cannot be all these things at one time."

clearly inviting the flood of requests that would follow, "is that I never felt a greater responsibility in my life. I have an opportunity which few human beings have, to help the influence for good that *Roots* inspires."

Although he would continue to regret the costs to both his private life and his writing ambitions, the role of a public figure was one for which the gregarious, always talkative Haley was uniquely suited. For one thing, he simply loved all of the attention, and the chance it gave him to meet and talk with all sorts of people, from the most distinguished dignitary to the ordinary person on the street.

"It was so interesting just to walk down the street with him," remembered A'lelia Bundles. "People would stop Alex wherever he went, and he was always so gracious. No matter what he was doing or how busy he was, he always stopped to say hello. He was just delighted that all those people wanted to meet him."

In the late 1980s, however, Haley began to steal time from his busy schedule of public appearances to research yet another major literary project: the *Roots*-style story of his father's family history. Haley acknowledged at the time that the book was in part the

Haley's paternal great-grandmother Queenie was the fair-skinned daughter (front, second from left) of a slave woman and a South Carolina plantation owner. At the end of his life, Haley was on the verge of completing a biography of Queenie as the final chapter in the Roots *saga.*

fulfillment of a long-overdue promise to his father, who had died not long before *Roots* was published. "He always wanted to know why I didn't write about his side of the family," Haley later confessed to an interviewer.

Based primarily on the life of his paternal grandmother, Queenie, the proposed saga required extensive genealogical research. This time, however, the information for which Haley was searching was better documented and easier to locate than that for the *Roots* project. But it was much more controversial.

Grandmother Queenie's grandfather James Jackson, Haley had discovered, was a white slaveholder and Civil War colonel of Irish descent. With *The Merging*, the book's proposed title at the time, Haley planned to trace the progression of his family from their preimmigration lives in 18th-century Ireland to their position as slaveholders in colonial America. Coming to grips with his own white, European ancestry was an idea that had fascinated Haley ever since he had first heard Malcolm X's angry sermons about the white slave masters' blood that most African-Americans carried within them.

But Haley would never be able to finish the story. On February 10, 1992, he died suddenly of a heart attack in Seattle, Washington, right in the middle of Black History Month.

In the days before his death, Haley had once again found himself at the center of public attention. In 1991, he received what he regarded as one of the two great honors of his literary career—along with his Pulitzer Prize—when his work was singled out for special recognition by his colleagues in the National Association of Black Journalists.

At the time of his death, NBC was already at work on the production of a three-part, six-hour miniseries of *Queen* (the new title for *The Merging*), to be aired the following year to coincide with the planned publication date of Haley's novel on the same topic. Already being touted by the network as "Roots: Part III," the program promised huge ratings and sustained public controversy, as the man who perhaps more than any other person had awakened the interest of black Americans in their African heritage now turned his attention to his roots in the white nation of Ireland.

The biggest controversy involving Haley, however, regarded the continuing legacy of his old friend Malcolm X. In November 1992, the gifted young director Spike Lee released his own tribute to the slain Black Muslim minister. Despite months of controversy and debate prior to the film's release, Lee's *Malcolm X* was based on the Haley/Malcolm X collaboration and remained surprisingly faithful to both the facts and the tone of the original book.

Though he would not live to see the completed film, Haley watched the arguments in the press with interest, particularly the spirited debate between Lee and activist/poet Amiri Baraka over which members of the African-American community were best suited to represent Malcolm X to the American public. Haley had always felt that the soul-searching and public debate that followed a book or film were even more important than the works themselves, and he viewed the fuss over Lee's movie with good-natured optimism. "I feel Malcolm would have liked both of them for their guts," Haley speculated to one reporter about the Lee-Baraka debate. Even after his death, Haley would remain one of the key players in the continuing debate over the Malcolm X legacy, as thousands of young Americans read *The Autobiography of Malcolm X* for the first time.

Haley often spoke with pride of the achievements of his brothers and sisters. His brother Julius became a navy architect; his sister Lois, a music teacher; and his brother George, a highly ranked Washington bureaucrat. In March 1990, George Haley (second from left) was sworn in as chairman of the U.S. Postal Rate Commission. Here George's family, including brother Alex (center) meet with President Bush.

Haley's huge estate in Norris, Tennessee, was a source of great satisfaction and great heartache, and at the time of his death he was already planning to sell it. Later, his family would have to sell the property in order to cover the author's debts—just as his grandmother Cynthia had been forced to sell her husband Will's beloved home in Henning more than 60 years earlier.

A few months after Haley's death, his family announced that the author's beloved estate in Norris was being sold at auction to cover debts that had remained unsettled at the time of his death. In one report, the combined claims against Haley's estate totaled $1.5 million. Tragically, most of the author's most cherished memorabilia were sold to the highest bidder, including his Pulitzer Prize, the original manuscripts of his books, and the crates full of precious souvenirs he had collected around the world while researching *Roots*.

Most, if not all, of Haley's literary effects would eventually end up on public display in museums or cultural centers, as Haley himself would have desired. According to Diana Lachatanere of New York's Schomburg Center for Research in Black Culture, however, the timing of Haley's death and the state of his affairs meant a great loss for the African-American community. "Black institutions can't compete," Ms. Lachatanere told a reporter for the *New York Times* after she and the representatives of many other black museums had been unable to match the bids of larger, predominantly white-controlled institutions. "They just don't have the resources. They just don't have the huge endowments or government funding."

Like his grandfather Will before him, Haley had always been good at making money and terrible at managing it. In developing his property in Norris, he had unfortunately continued the habit that had caused him so much embarrassment years earlier in Africa—signing his name to checks and just assuming that the work would be done and the bills would be covered without his further attention.

But Haley had been having problems with the estate for some time. In the years before his death, he had begun to realize that the costs of running his palatial home were beginning to exceed both the money and the time that he had to invest in it. Reluctantly, he had already begun to make plans to sell it. "I've had great fun creating it," he confessed to one interviewer. "But it's really something I have to worry about all the time, and it's one more thing that keeps me from writing."

The turmoil over his home in Norris cost Haley dearly during his final days. Trying to keep up with his mounting debts, he revved up his schedule of public appearances. He spoke to more than 50 groups around the country during 1991, in addition to his now intensive work on *Queen* and the continuing hassles with the estate. It was a pace that the 70-year-old author could not possibly sustain for long. "Part of the reason Alex isn't with us," reflected A'Lelia Bundles several months after Haley's death, "is that he simply ran himself ragged."

True to style, Haley told an interviewer only a few weeks before his death that both *Queen* and the Walker novel would be published by the end of the year. At the time of his death, however, *Queen* remained incomplete, and the Walker manuscript was still waiting to be written. The chapters for *Henning*, Haley's long-awaited novel about his childhood in Tennessee, were essentially intact, many of them having already appeared in print as separate stories in magazines. But Haley had shelved the project years earlier and had never returned to the final editing of the book.

It was in one of those chapters, "Home to Henning," that Haley told the curious tale of Pete Gause, an ambitious young black man who had left the sleepy town to seek fame and fortune "Up North." After several years away, Pete had finally made it big and returned to visit his mother, Fannie. In the story's most dramatic scene, the proud, aloof Pete, embarrassed and angered by the poverty and ignorance to which he had returned, ripped his mother's old cast-iron stove from the wall and angrily hurled it from the back porch.

Haley's work continues to inspire and to challenge millions of readers and viewers around the world, of all colors and nationalities. "I think we as people—and I am talking about the world—badly need uplifting. We all have a lineage and forefathers. If I have become a symbol of the shared search for ancestral roots, then indeed I am blessed."

After her son's all-too-brief visit, Sister Fannie tried in vain to interest her friends in the shiny new oven with which Pete had immediately replaced the other. Instead, the townsfolk chose to congregate together at the fence behind her house, admiring the remains of the bulky old hunk of metal that the Gause boy had tossed so unceremoniously into the yard.

"For years to come, in fact, black people kept on walking up to see Sister Fannie's broken old stove," Haley wrote. "And the reason was that just looking at it gave the black people of Henning a might big feeling of pride."

With typical good humor, Haley had summed up his stalled literary career in the battered remains of Fannie Gause's old black stove. Though he longed throughout his final years to create something new and magnificent for himself and his race, he could never finally escape his country's fascination with the dark, tormented, and at times triumphant history that *Malcolm X* had suggested and that *Roots* had finally uncovered for everyone to see.

Before *Roots* was released, many people in the media feared that it would polarize black and white Americans, unleashing racial tensions that would damage the struggle for community and equality. Haley believed otherwise, and *Roots*, despite all the controversies and criticism, promises to remain one of the great, enduring works of black culture and American history.

"To me," wrote Haley in evaluating the impact of his work, "the overwhelming affirmation of *Roots* can be explained only by something that is beyond ordinary comprehension, something spiritual. I think we as people—and I am talking about the world— badly need uplifting. We all have lineage and forefathers. If I have become a symbol of the shared search for ancestral roots, then indeed I am blessed."

APPENDIX: SELECTED BIBLIOGRAPHY

BOOKS
1965 *The Autobiography of Malcolm X*. New York: Grove Press.
1976 *Roots: The Saga of an American Family*. New York: Doubleday.
1988 *A Different Kind of Christmas*. New York: Doubleday.

ARTICLES
1960 "Mr. Muhammad Speaks." *Reader's Digest*, March, 100–104.
1964 "In 'Uncle Tom' Are Our Guilt and Hope." *New York Times Magazine*, March 1.
1972 "What Roots Means to Me." *Reader's Digest*, May, 73–75.
1982 "Sea Islanders, Strong-willed Survivors Face Their Uncertain Futures Together." *Smithsonian*, October, 88–97.
1983 "Home to Henning." *Reader's Digest*, May, 81–90.
1983 "The Christmas That Gave Me Roots." *McCalls*, December.

CHRONOLOGY

———— •❀• ————

1921   Alexander Palmer Haley born on August 11 in Ithaca, New York

1925   First learns about his African ancestors

1937   Graduates from high school; enrolls at Elizabeth City Teachers College in Elizabeth City, North Carolina

1939   Leaves college to join the Coast Guard

1941   Marries Nannie Branch

1949   Sells three stories to *Coronet* magazine; promoted to chief journalist and restationed to office job in New York City

1954   Publication of his first article in the *Reader's Digest*

1959   Retires from the Coast Guard and settles in New York City; meets Malcolm X for the first time

1960   "Mr. Muhammad Speaks" is published in the *Reader's Digest*

1962   Interviews Miles Davis for *Playboy* (in the first of his series on prominent black Americans); interviews Malcolm X for *Playboy*

1963   Begins work on *The Autobiography of Malcolm X*

1964   Signs with Doubleday to write *Before This Anger*, the story of his family's rise from slavery; marries Juliette Collins

1965   Malcolm X is assassinated; *The Autobiography of Malcolm X* is published

1966   First travels to Gambia

1967   Learns about his ancestor Kunta Kinte from a griot in the village of Juffure, Gambia

1976   *Roots* is published

1977   "Roots: The Triumph of an American Family" airs on television; Haley receives the Pulitzer Prize; sues Doubleday; Haley is sued for plagiarism by novelists May Wallace and Harold Courlander

1983   Buys a 127-acre estate in Norris, Tennessee

1988   Publication of *A Different Kind of Christmas*

1992   Dies of a heart attack on February 10 in Seattle, Washington

FURTHER READING

Aptheker, Herbert. *Afro-American History: The Modern Era*. New York: Citadel Press, 1971.

Baker, Houston A., Jr. *Black Literature in America*. New York: McGraw-Hill, 1971.

Courlander, Harold. *The African*. New York: Crown, 1977.

Davis, Arthur P. *From the Dark Tower: Afro-American Writers, 1900 to 1960*. Washington, D.C.: Howard University Press, 1982.

Franklin, John Hope. *From Slavery to Freedom: A History of Negro Americans*. New York: Knopf, 1980.

Goldman, Peter. *The Death and Life of Malcolm X*. Champaign: University of Illinois Press, 1979.

Haley, Alex, and David Stevens. *Queen*. New York: Morrow, 1993.

Lincoln, C. Eric. *The Black Muslims in America*. Boston: Beacon Press, 1973.

Meier, August, and Elliot Rudwick, eds. *The Making of Black America*. New York: Atheneum, 1969.

Rummel, Jack. *Malcom X*. New York: Chelsea House, 1989.

Walker, Margaret. *Jubilee*. New York: Bantam, 1975.

INDEX

PICTURE CREDITS

———— ❧ ————

DAVID SHIRLEY is a freelance writer living in New York City. He is the author of *Satchel Paige* in Chelsea House's BLACK AMERICANS OF ACHIEVEMENT series and *A Good Death*. He is also a contributing editor at *Option* magazine.

NATHAN IRVIN HUGGINS, one of America's leading scholars in the field of black studies, helped select the titles for the BLACK AMERICANS OF ACHIEVEMENT series, for which he also served as senior consulting editor. He was the W. E. B. Du Bois Professor of History and of Afro-American Studies at Harvard University and the director of the W. E. B. Du Bois Institute for Afro-American Research at Harvard. He received his doctorate from Harvard in 1962 and returned there as a professor in 1980 after teaching at Columbia University, the University of Massachusetts, Lake Forest College, and the California State University, Long Beach. He was the author of four books and dozens of articles, including *Black Odyssey: The Afro-American Ordeal in Slavery*, *The Harlem Renaissance*, and *Slave and Citizen: The Life of Frederick Douglass*, and was associated with the Children's Television Workshop, National Public Radio, the Boston Athenaeum, the Museum of Afro-American History, the Howard Thurman Educational Trust, and Upward Bound. Professor Huggins died in 1989, at the age of 62, in Cambridge, Massachusetts.